ENDORSEMENTS

"What I love about Steve Lawson's books is that he writes as a preacher, with a keen eye and ear for details that show what a vital role great preaching has played in the advance of the gospel, the growth and strengthening of the church, and the collective testimony of the Evangelical movement. This volume on George Whitefield is another superb example of Dr. Lawson's approach to history and biography. He highlights the key doctrinal nuances, character qualities, natural talents, and spiritual gifts that help explain why Whitefield was such a powerful preacher and such a monumental figure in church history. The book is written in an engaging, personal way that brings Whitefield to life. It's hard to put a book like this down."

—DR. JOHN MACARTHUR
Pastor, Grace Community Church
President, The Master's College and Seminary
Sun Valley, California

"Effective evangelism is humanly impossible. To take truth from the Bible, get it into your heart, cause it to burst into flames of love, and then carry its living coals into another heart—no man has the power to do this. It requires an anointing from heaven. God gave that anointing to George Whitefield and used him to ignite thousands of souls. Steven Lawson draws us close to feel the fire in this stirring and informative book. May many read it and cry up to heaven for the flame to descend again!"

—DR. JOEL R. BEEKE
President, Puritan Reformed Theological Seminary
Grand Rapids, Michigan

"When Whitefield came to town, everything stopped, everyone listened. And what did they hear? As Dr. Steven Lawson makes clear, they heard the gospel plainly, powerfully, and persuasively proclaimed. Read this book and you'll learn the amazing story of George Whitefield—and then pray that God will use this book to raise up Whitefields in our day."

—DR. STEPHEN J. NICHOLS
Research Professor of Christianity and Culture
Lancaster Bible College
Lancaster, Pennsylvania

"There is little doubt that George Whitefield is one of the most remarkable preachers in the history of Christianity: his preaching was central to the Great Awakening that refashioned British society on both sides of the Atlantic; it gripped the mind and imagination of so many in his era, and led to the conversion of thousands; and most importantly, it set forth plainly and faithfully the biblical gospel. To be reminded of all of this and much more by Dr. Lawson's new study of Whitefield as a preacher is vital in our day, when far too many professing Christians disparage preaching and are questioning key facets of the gospel of Christ that Whitefield preached."

—DR. MICHAEL A. G. HAYKIN
Professor of Church History and Biblical Spirituality
The Southern Baptist Theological Seminary
Louisville, Kentucky

The Evangelistic Zeal *of*

George Whitefield

The Long Line of Godly Men Profiles
Series editor, Steven J. Lawson

The Expository Genius of John Calvin
by Steven J. Lawson

The Unwavering Resolve of Jonathan Edwards
by Steven J. Lawson

The Mighty Weakness of John Knox
by Douglas Bond

The Gospel Focus of Charles Spurgeon
by Steven J. Lawson

The Heroic Boldness of Martin Luther
by Steven J. Lawson

The Poetic Wonder of Isaac Watts
by Douglas Bond

A **Long Line of Godly Men** Profile

The Evangelistic Zeal *of*

George Whitefield

STEVEN J. LAWSON

IR *Reformation Trust*   A DIVISION OF LIGONIER MINISTRIES, ORLANDO, FL

The Evangelistic Zeal of George Whitefield

© 2013 by Steven J. Lawson

Published by Reformation Trust Publishing
a division of Ligonier Ministries
421 Ligonier Court, Sanford, FL 32771
Ligonier.org   ReformationTrust.com

Printed in Crawfordsville, Indiana
RR Donnelley and Sons
May 2014
First edition, second printing

Cover design: Chris Larson
Cover illustration: Kent Barton
Interior design and typeset: Katherine Lloyd, The DESK

Scripture quotations are from *The Holy Bible, King James Version*. Public domain.

Library of Congress Cataloging-in-Publication Data
Lawson, Steven J.
The evangelistic zeal of George Whitefield / Steven J. Lawson.
    pages cm. -- (A long line of godly men profile)
Includes bibliographical references and index.
ISBN-13: 978-1-56769-363-8
ISBN-10: 1-56769-363-6
    1. Whitefield, George, 1714-1770. 2. Preaching--History--18th century. I. Title.
BX9225.W4L39 2014
269'.2092--dc23
                                    2013037124

To Kent Stainback,
a devoted and faithful friend
whose passion for the gospel
reflects the evangelistic zeal
of George Whitefield and
whose spiritual influence
has helped launch
OnePassion Ministries

TABLE OF CONTENTS

Followers Worthy to be Followed

Down through the centuries, God has providentially raised up a long line of godly men, those whom He has mightily used at strategic moments in church history. These valiant soldiers of the cross have come from all walks of life—from the ivy-covered halls of elite schools to the dusty back rooms of tradesmen's shops. They have arisen from all points of this world—from highly visible venues in densely populated cities to obscure hamlets in remote places. Yet despite these differences, these pivotal figures have had much in common.

Each man possessed not only an unwavering faith in the Lord Jesus Christ, but more than that, each of these stalwarts of the faith held deep convictions in the God-exalting truths known as the doctrines of grace. Though they differed in secondary matters of theology, they stood shoulder-to-shoulder in championing these biblical teachings that magnify the sovereign grace of God in salvation. They upheld the foundational truth that "salvation is of the Lord" (Jonah 2:9; Ps. 3:8).

Any survey of church history reveals that those who have embraced these Reformed truths have been granted extraordinary confidence in their God. Far from paralyzing these spiritual giants, the doctrines of grace kindled within their hearts a reverential awe for God that humbled their souls before His throne. The truths of sovereign grace emboldened these men to rise up and advance the cause of Christ on the earth. With an enlarged vision of His saving grace, they stepped forward boldly and accomplished the work of ten, even twenty men. They arose with wings like eagles and soared over their times. The doctrines of grace empowered them to serve God in their divinely appointed hour, leaving a godly influence upon future generations.

This Long Line of Godly Men Profile series highlights key figures in the agelong procession of sovereign-grace men. The purpose of this series is to explore how these figures used their God-given gifts and abilities to impact their times and further the kingdom of heaven. Because they were courageous followers of Christ, their examples are worthy of emulation today.

This volume focuses upon the great English evangelist George Whitefield. In the eighteenth century, a day plagued by lifeless orthodoxy, Whitefield burst onto the scene with power and passion. In a day marked by great spiritual decline, Whitefield preached with a supernatural unction and intense boldness that became the primary catalyst in ushering in two major revivals simultaneously, one in the British Isles and the other in the American colonies. As the Lord empowered him, Whitefield's clarion voice called men and women to the foot of the cross. Perhaps no gospel herald has ever been so effectively used in so many places over such an extended period of time. For these and countless more reasons, George Whitefield remains eminently worthy to be profiled in this series.

May the Lord greatly use this book to embolden a new generation of leaders so that they, like Whitefield, might leave an indelible mark on this world for God. Through this profile, may you be strengthened to walk in a manner worthy of your calling. May you be filled with Scripture and, thereby, zealous in your evangelistic endeavors for the exaltation of Christ and the advance of His kingdom.

Soli Deo gloria
—Steven J. Lawson
Series editor

Lightning From a Cloudless Sky

The gospel was to be recovered for nations and God had prepared Whitefield to preach it.[1]

—Iain H. Murray

If I could be anyone in church history, I would be George Whitefield. I say this not because of his great oratorical skills or his worldwide fame, but primarily because of his consuming evangelistic zeal. Preeminently, Whitefield has instilled within me a passion for preaching.

Through Martin Luther, I have been motivated to strive for greater boldness for the truth. From John Calvin, I have gained a greater desire to preach the Scripture in a sequential, expositional manner. Through Jonathan Edwards, I have been challenged in terms of discipline in Christian living. From Charles Spurgeon, I have learned the necessity of an intense gospel focus in every sermon. But when it comes to George

Whitefield, I have been captivated by his unmatched zeal in proclaiming the gospel message to the ends of the earth.

In this book, it is my desire to unveil the heart of a man who burned to accomplish the work of God. My sincere hope is that George Whitefield's example will rekindle your passion for taking the name of Christ to the nations. I pray that this book will move a new generation of gospel preachers to advance into the fields of the world white for harvest. But before we examine the life and ministry of this extraordinary man, let me first establish the historical setting in which he lived.

The eighteenth century for the English-speaking world was a monumental period of spiritual awakening. Martyn Lloyd-Jones called this time "the greatest manifestation of the power of the Holy Spirit since apostolic days."[2] This era proved to be an unprecedented season of evangelistic endeavor and spiritual renewal. Its effects spanned two continents and were especially dramatic given the spiritual lethargy that permeated the church and culture of that day. This season proved to be nothing less than a "second reformation."

Since the seventeenth century, gospel preaching had waxed cold throughout Europe, but especially in England. The state church was already in spiritual decline. Presbyterianism had weakened, and the General Baptists began a slippery descent from Arminianism to Unitarianism.

Several factors caused these days of drought. Many churches no longer required a regenerate church membership and were careless in whom they admitted to the Lord's table. Puritanism suffered a devastating blow when Parliament passed the Act of Uniformity in 1662, which permanently divided the Church of England from all other Protestants, thereafter known as Dissenters.[3] Under Charles II, this decree determined a more Catholic-like form of public prayers, the priesthood, the sacraments, and other rites in the Church of England. Puritan ministers were required to abandon their original ordinations and be reordained under this new form of the state church.

This brewing crisis came to a head on August 24, 1662, St. Bartholomew's Day, when two thousand Puritan ministers were ejected from their churches. In a single day, the greatest generation of gospel preachers was discharged from the pulpit and forbidden to preach. These Puritan ministers suffered even greater restrictions with the passing of the Conventicle Act in 1664. They were banned from preaching in the fields or conducting private worship services in the homes of parishioners. Further restriction came with the Five Mile Act in 1665, which barred ejected ministers from coming within five miles of their former churches or any city or town.

This persecution was lifted in 1689 by the Toleration Act under William and Mary, but by this time, most of the leading Puritan ministers had already died. Forbidden from being buried in English churchyards, many Puritan pastors were entombed in a separate Nonconformist cemetery in Bunhill Fields, outside of London. Included in this despised cemetery were such notables as John Bunyan, John Owen, Isaac Watts, and Thomas Goodwin. Considered outcasts and deemed unworthy, these men of God were buried outside the city limits. Puritan influence had ebbed sharply.

At the same time, many highly esteemed Anglican pulpits taught a moralistic, legalistic corruption of justification by faith. This doctrinal decline left the English church with little appetite for the preaching of the Word. Any burden for the lost had waned. Like the Apostles in the Garden of Gethsemane, English ministers had left off watching and were lulled into a deep sleep. Biblical convictions were replaced with the prevailing secular philosophies. There was a virtual famine in the land for the hearing of God's Word.

It was into this spiritual void that God raised up the English evangelist George Whitefield. Like lightning from a cloudless sky, Whitefield stepped onto the world stage as the most prolific herald of the gospel since the days of the New Testament. God empowered Whitefield to become a blazing lamp set on a hill in the midst of Satan's empire of darkness.

This powerful figure of unusual gospel fervor stood at the headwaters of an Evangelical resurgence. His thundering voice was the catalyst for spiritual awakening, as his preaching took the British Isles by storm and electrified the American colonies. By his evangelistic zeal, he stoked the flames of revival until they spread to the hearts of countless men and women. It can be argued that by his preaching, the British Isles were saved from the equivalent of the French Revolution. And on the other side of the Atlantic, a nation would be birthed in the wake of his gospel proclamation.

Given the many ailments plaguing the church today, this present generation needs a strong dose of George Whitefield. As we look at modern Christianity, there is much for which to be thankful, especially in light of the Reformed resurgence of recent years. However, it has become a trend for many in this movement to retreat into a Calvinistic cloister, having little impact upon the world around them. Whitefield, through his intense engagement with the world and fervent proclamation of the gospel, has much to teach us concerning what desperately needs to be recovered.

We have too many mild-mannered apologists lecturing in pulpits today. The need of this hour is for red-hot *proclaimers* of God and His saving grace, not for mere philosophical explainers. It is all too easy to become ensnared in the web of social and political concerns that displaces our primary duty to preach Christ. What needs to be recovered in this hour is Whitefield's deep belief in the sovereign grace of God, coupled with a zealous desire to call the lost to repentance and faith in Christ. Whitefield saw that the greatest need of humanity is to have right standing before God. As Whitefield fulfilled his God-given call to passionately summon a lost and dying world to believe in the gospel, so must we do the same.

■ ■ ■

Before we proceed to consider George Whitefield, I must thank the publishing team at Reformation Trust for their commitment to this Long Line of Godly Men Profile series. I remain grateful to Chris Larson, who has been instrumental in overseeing this series. I remain thankful for the ongoing influence of my former professor and current friend, Dr. R. C. Sproul.

I am indebted to Christ Fellowship Baptist Church of Mobile, Alabama, which I serve as senior pastor. I cannot imagine that any other pastor has ever received as much encouragement to serve Christ on such a far-reaching scale as I have. I am extremely grateful for the support of my fellow elders and congregation, who continuously encourage me in my extended ministry abroad.

I want to express my gratitude for my executive assistant, Kay Allen, who typed this document, and Dustin Benge and Keith Phillips, fellow pastors at Christ Fellowship, who helped prepare this manuscript.

I thank God for my family and for their support in my life and ministry. My wife, Anne, and our four children, Andrew, James, Grace Anne, and John, remain pillars of strength for me.

May the Lord use Whitefield's example, whether you are a layperson or a preacher, to embolden your own commitment to the cause of Christ and to the furtherance of His gospel. In these days, when there is a crying need for boldness both in the pulpit and the pew, may we see the restoration of Christ's church to her pristine purity through a new reformation.

—Steven J. Lawson
Mobile, Alabama
August 2013

CHAPTER ONE

A Force
for the Gospel

Other men seem to be only half-alive, but Whitefield was all life, fire, wing, force. My own model, if I may have such a thing in due subordination to my Lord, is George Whitefield. With unequal footsteps must I follow his glorious track.[1]

—CHARLES SPURGEON

R eaching from one side of the Atlantic to the other, the expansive ministry of George Whitefield (1714–1770) remains unmatched to this day. Relentless in drive and fervent in soul, this "Grand Itinerant" was the chosen instrument in the hands of our sovereign God for the ingathering of untold thousands into His kingdom. Reaching the British Isles from London to Edinburgh and the American colonies from Boston to Savannah, this anointed herald of the gospel was the force behind the British Evangelical movement and the First Great Awakening.

There had been other open-air preachers before Whitefield. In the thirteenth century, the Waldensians circulated throughout central Europe propagating the gospel. During the fourteenth century, a band of brave preachers known as the Lollards were sent out by John Wycliffe (c. 1320–1384) to proclaim Christ in the villages and fields of England. Howell Harris (1714–1773), a contemporary of Whitefield, had preached in the open air of Wales. But *never* had there been anyone like Whitefield in terms of scope and power. In fact, not since the first-century missionary journeys of the Apostle Paul had such evangelistic preaching been taken so directly to the masses of the world.

In his thirty-four years of ministry, Whitefield preached some eighteen thousand sermons, often to multiplied thousands. If informal messages are included, such as in private homes, this number easily increases to thirty thousand sermons, perhaps more. Three sermons a day were common; four were not uncommon. Conservative estimates are that he spoke a thousand times every year for more than thirty years. In America alone, it is estimated that eighty percent of the colonists heard him preach. This means Whitefield was seen by far more American settlers than was George Washington. Whitefield's name was more widely recognized by colonial Americans than any living person's except for those of British royalty. It is believed that Whitefield preached to more than ten million people over the course of his ministry, a staggering number.

Making seven demanding trips to America, Whitefield crossed the Atlantic Ocean thirteen times for the express purpose of preaching the gospel. He spent almost three years of his life on a ship en route to preach. In all, about eight years of his life were spent in America. He made fifteen trips to Scotland, two to Ireland, and one each to Gibraltar, Bermuda, and the Netherlands. Of this unparalleled outreach, Whitefield could truly say, "The whole world is now my parish. Wheresoever my Master calls me, I am ready to go and preach the everlasting gospel."[2] Since the time of the Apostles, the annals of church history record no other individual who possessed such gospel ambition and relentless determination.

Whitefield's contemporaries never encountered his like. The great English hymn writer William Cowper marveled that in Whitefield, "The apostolical times seem to have returned upon us."[3] Another famed hymn writer, John Newton, stated, "As a preacher, if any man were to ask me who was second-best I had ever heard, I should be at some loss; but in regard to the first, Mr. Whitefield so far exceeds every other man of my time that I should be at no loss to say."[4] Yet another renowned hymn writer, Augustus Toplady, praised him as "the prince of preachers, the apostle of the English Empire, and the most useful minister that has perhaps been produced since the days of the apostles."[5]

The greatest preachers of history have been the strongest admirers of Whitefield. J. C. Ryle, a noted preacher and author, asserted, "I believe no English preacher has ever possessed such a combination of excellent qualifications as Whitefield. . . .

Whitefield, I repeat my opinion, stands alone."[6] The undisputed Prince of Preachers, Charles Spurgeon, testified: "Often as I have read his life, I am conscious of distinct quickening whenever I turn to it. He *lived*. Other men seem to be only half-alive; but Whitefield was all life, fire, wing, force. My own model, if I may have such a thing in due subordination to my Lord, is George Whitefield; but with unequal footsteps must I follow his glorious track."[7] Spurgeon's only mentor in preaching was Whitefield. On his personal copy of Whitefield's sermons, he wrote, "C. H. Spurgeon, who admires Whitefield as Chief of Preachers."[8]

The famed expositor Martyn Lloyd-Jones spoke in awe of this celebrated preacher: "George Whitefield is beyond any question the greatest English preacher of all time. . . . This man was simply a phenomenon."[9] Ian Paisley, founder of the Free Presbyterian Church of Ulster, asserted, "Without a doubt, George Whitefield was the greatest preacher of his or any subsequent generation."[10]

Those who are students of preaching place Whitefield at the head of their list. Historian Edwin C. Dargan said, "The history of preaching since the apostles does not contain a greater or worthier name than that of George Whitefield."[11] Yale historian Harry Stout wrote that Whitefield was "America's first cultural hero." He added, "Before Whitefield, there was no unifying intercolonial person or event. . . . But by 1750 virtually every American loved and admired Whitefield and saw him as their champion."[12]

As with Moses in Egypt, Paul in Rome, or Luther in

Wittenberg, God places His chosen servants in decisive eras of history when a voice is needed to advance the cause of His kingdom. In the powerful revivals of the eighteenth century, a season of spiritual renewal unlike any in church history, Whitefield was this voice, rousing the church from its spiritual slumber and fortifying her faith in the living God.

What was it that made Whitefield such an effective evangelist of the gospel of Jesus Christ? From the divine perspective, God sovereignly chose to use George Whitefield simply because it pleased Him. But humanly speaking, what God-given virtues qualified this tireless preacher to be so mightily used? Before we address these questions, let us first consider an overview of this extraordinary man.

Though he was arguably the greatest preacher of the Christian era, Whitefield ironically remains an enigma to most. A survey of his life and exploits becomes necessary because, as Lloyd-Jones once said, Whitefield is "the most neglected man in the whole of church history."[13] Lloyd-Jones further lamented, "Whitefield is an unknown man and the great story concerning him is something that people never seem to have heard."[14] For this reason, let us now hear the story of this unsung hero, the "Father of Evangelicalism."

BIRTH AND NEW BIRTH

Born on December 16, 1714, in Gloucester, England, George Whitefield was the sixth and youngest son of Thomas and

Elizabeth Whitefield, the owners of the Bell Inn. His father died when he was only two years old. He was raised by his mother until she remarried when he was eight. Unfortunately, this remarriage was not a happy one, and eventually ended in divorce. In such unrest, George became involved in stealing, lying, fighting, and cursing. He had a knowledge of sin during these formative years, but had no knowledge of Christ.

The real interest of young Whitefield lay in the theatrical stage. A born actor and orator, George entertained the guests of the inn with his dramatics. He developed speaking abilities and powers of elocution that would be enhanced and used in his future ministry. Possessing a remarkable mind, sixteen-year-old George began reading the Greek New Testament and gained a proficiency in Latin. Throughout this time, though, his restless soul remained unconverted.

At age eighteen, Whitefield entered Pembroke College at Oxford University. To subsidize his education, he worked as a servitor, one who attended the needs of the wealthier students—cleaning their rooms, doing laundry, and preparing their meals. Amid the mounting demands of school and struggling with a guilty conscience, Whitefield ardently pursued a right standing before God. In a desperate spiritual struggle, he prayed three times a day and fasted, but found no peace for his troubled soul.

Near the end of Whitefield's first year at Oxford, Charles Wesley (1707–1788), the future hymn writer, introduced him to a small group of students known as the "Oxford Holy

Club." Included in this group was Charles' brother, John Wesley (1703–1791), and ten others who met to pursue religiously moral lives. Despite their rigid discipline in Bible reading, study, prayer, fasting, and service, not one of these young students was converted. So stringent was Whitefield in his self-righteous efforts to earn salvation that his severe discipline caused him to suffer a lifelong physical weakness.

Urgently searching for acceptance by God, Whitefield was given a book by Charles Wesley in the spring of 1735. It was a book on the new birth, called *The Life of God in the Soul of Man*, by Henry Scougal. He learned that the way of salvation was not by his own religious works but by divine regeneration. Under tremendous agony of conviction, he realized, "I must be born again or be damned!"[15] At age twenty-one, Whitefield was regenerated by the Holy Spirit, and placed his faith in Christ. He confessed:

> A man may go to church, say his prayers, receive the Sacrament, and yet . . . not be a Christian. . . . Lord, if I am not a Christian, if I am not a real one, for Jesus Christ's sake, show me what Christianity is, that I may not be damned at last. I read a little further, and the cheat was discovered; O, says the author, they that know any thing of religion know it is a vital union with the Son of God, Christ formed in the heart; O what a ray of divine life did then break in upon my poor soul.[16]

An agonizing five-year search for acceptance by God was now realized. Being born again would be the repeated theme of his entire future ministry. He stated:

> God was pleased at length to remove the heavy load, to enable me to lay hold on His dear Son by a living faith, and, by giving me the Spirit of adoption, to seal me, as I humbly hope, even to the day of everlasting redemption. But oh! With what joy—joy unspeakable—even joy that was full of, and big with glory, was my soul filled, when the weight of sin went off.[17]

Soundly converted, Whitefield was gripped with an all-consuming desire to know Christ more intimately. In humble submission, he began reading the Bible on his knees and devouring Matthew Henry's *Exposition of the Old and New Testament*. This saturation with biblical truth immediately grounded him in the Reformed faith, which would profoundly shape his preaching.

The Wesleys, still unconverted, departed for the mission field in the American colony of Georgia, leaving Whitefield the leader of the Holy Club. With flaming zeal in his soul, he evangelized his fellow students and placed new believers into small-group Bible studies. This strict discipline in Bible study led many to label the members of the Holy Club with the derisive term "Methodists."

FROM PULPITS TO FIELDS

Upon graduating from Oxford in 1736, Whitefield returned to Gloucester, where he was ordained as a deacon in the Church of England. "I can call heaven and earth to witness," Whitefield recalled, "that when the bishop laid his hand upon me, I gave myself up to be a martyr for Him who hung upon the cross for me."[18] But there was something unusual that God had in store for him.

Almost immediately, Whitefield sensed God's call to preach, and one week later he delivered his first sermon in Saint Mary de Crypt Church, Gloucester, where he had been baptized. When he returned to Oxford for further studies, the compulsion to preach grew even stronger. For the next two months, Whitefield felt drawn to fill pulpits in London. It was instantly recognized that this young preacher possessed unusual homiletic gifts. The sanctuaries were filled to hear this young preaching phenomenon.

Unexpectedly, correspondence came from John and Charles Wesley in Georgia, urging Whitefield to help in their new missionary work. "Upon reading this, my heart leaped within me, and, as it were, echoed to the call,"[19] he said. He was determined to sail to the American colonies and help in this new endeavor. Before leaving, Whitefield returned to Gloucester to say farewell to his family and took the opportunity to preach, again to swelling crowds that gathered under the great power of the Word.

Returning to London, Whitefield was ready to make his inaugural journey to the American colonies, but his ship was detained. Taking full advantage of the delay, Whitefield accepted invitations to preach in Gloucester, Bristol, Bath, and London. Wherever he went, news spread of this young pulpit prodigy. Church buildings were packed, hearts were stirred, and souls were converted. In a day known for dry, moralistic sermons that lacked any element of emotion, Whitefield came with fiery proclamations of the gospel that awakened people to their need for Christ. This unknown twenty-three-year-old evangelist was suddenly widely acclaimed. He wrote:

> The tide of popularity now began to run high. In a short time, I could no longer walk on foot as usual, but was constrained to go in a coach, from place to place, to avoid the hosannas of the multitude. They grew quite extravagant in their applauses; and, had it not been for my compassionate High Priest, popularity would have destroyed me. I used to plead with Him to take me by the hand and lead me unhurt through this fiery furnace. He heard my request, and gave me to see the vanity of all commendations but His own. . . . I would be so overpowered with a sense of God's infinite Majesty that I would be constrained to throw myself on the ground, and offer my soul as a blank in His hands, to write on it what He pleased.[20]

During Whitefield's first eighteen months of preaching, his initial labors were nothing short of astonishing. He burst onto the scene proclaiming the Word with greater fervency than had been heard before, and it stirred the souls of thousands in England out of their spiritual lethargy. Overflowing congregations were eager to hear him preach.

Finally, on December 28, 1737, the *Whittaker* was ready to depart for the American colony of Georgia. Though adverse weather further delayed its departure, Whitefield at last arrived in Savannah, Georgia, on May 7, 1738, only to discover that John Wesley had left the colony under indictment by a grand jury. The mission work was in complete shambles. As Whitefield surveyed the scene, he saw a great number of orphans and felt compelled to build an orphanage. Such an ambitious project would require substantial funds, however. In order to raise these necessary resources, Whitefield sailed back to England on August 28, arriving three months later on November 30.

Upon his return, Whitefield discovered the Wesleys had been converted and had assumed the leadership of this new, emerging movement known as Methodism. As Whitefield and the Wesleys preached, this dynamic trio emphasized the necessity of the new birth. They even insisted that many ministers in the Church of England were unconverted, causing no small stir. This daring assertion prompted many church leaders to resist their work. Vicious pamphlets were circulated in opposition to them and rumors spread, smearing Whitefield's name. Church doors were closed to him, forcing a bold new strategy. He would bypass church buildings altogether and preach in the open air.

On February 17, 1739, Whitefield preached for the first time outdoors at Kingswood, in a field on the outskirts of Bristol. He stood on a little hill in the countryside and preached to a relatively small gathering of coal miners and their families, some two hundred in attendance. Whitefield declared the saving grace of Jesus Christ, and those in attendance were struck by the power of the gospel. He remarked on that event:

> Having no righteousness of their own to renounce, they were glad to hear of a Jesus who was a friend of publicans, and came not to call the righteous, but sinners to repentance. The first discovery of their being affected was to see the white gutters made by their tears which plentifully fell down their black cheeks, as they came out of their coal pits. Hundreds and hundreds of them were soon brought under deep convictions, which, as the event proved, happily ended in a sound and thorough conversion. The change was visible to all, though numbers chose to impute it to anything, rather than the finger of God.[21]

This first success in open-air preaching proved to be the turning point not only for Whitefield's ministry but, in many ways, for evangelicalism in general. He preached wherever he could draw a crowd, whether in open fields, bustling marketplaces, churchyard cemeteries, or aboard seafaring ships. Whitefield's own accounts of his initial London meetings are quite remarkable. His *Journals* is filled with entries that chronicle explosive crowds flocking to hear his gospel message. It is estimated that Whitefield preached to around 650,000 people per month during 1739, which equals around twenty-two thousand people per day.[22] Recounting one sermon, he wrote:

> Preached in the evening at a place called Mayfair, near Hyde Park Corner. The congregation, I believe, consisted of near eighty thousand people. It was, by far, the largest I ever preached to yet. In the time of my prayer, there was a little noise; but they kept a deep silence during my whole discourse. A high and very commodious scaffold was erected for me to stand upon; and though I was weak in myself, yet God strengthened me to speak so loud, that most could hear, and so powerfully, that most, I believe, could feel. All love, all glory be to God through Christ![23]

Armed with this new approach, Whitefield resolved, "Field-preaching is my plan; in this I am carried as on eagles' wings."[24] He further asserted: "It is good to go into the highways and hedges. Field-preaching, field-preaching forever!"[25] He was unfazed by opposition: "My preaching in the fields may displease some timorous, bigoted men, but I am thoroughly persuaded it pleases God, and why should I fear anything else?"[26] So attached to preaching in the field was Whitefield that he once remarked, "Oh that I may die in the field!"[27] Within weeks, Whitefield was preaching multiple times per week to crowds numbering in the thousands.

On March 25, five weeks after his first open-air sermon, Whitefield stood before an crowd of twenty-three thousand to deliver his final sermon at Bristol. Reflecting on this momentous occasion, Whitefield remarked:

> As . . . I had just begun to be an extempore preacher, it often occasioned many inward conflicts. Sometimes, when twenty thousand people were before me, I had not, in my own apprehension, a word to say either to God or them. But I never was totally deserted, and frequently . . . so assisted, that I knew by happy experience what our Lord meant by saying, "Out of His belly shall flow rivers of living water" [John 7:38]. The open firmament above me, the prospect of the adjacent fields, with the sight of thousands and thousands, some in coaches, some on horseback, and some in the trees, and at times all affected and drenched in tears together, to which sometimes was added the solemnity of the approaching evening, was almost too much for, and quite overcame me.[28]

This initial success provoked much opposition. Feeling threatened, the bishop of Bristol accused Whitefield of "pretending" to have received "extraordinary revelations and gifts of the Holy Ghost," which the bishop called "a very horrid thing."[29] Such resistance would not deter the young evangelist. With mounting confidence, he returned to London in order to preach in the open air. He preached in Moorfields, a public park, to thousands gathered for amusement. He preached at Kennington Common to a multitude of thirty thousand, where many were deeply convicted and turned to Christ. Believing God was with him in the open fields, Whitefield preached at Hampstead Heath and Bedford to swelling numbers. A staggering eighty thousand people gathered to hear him at Hyde Park. His outdoor preaching continued at Cirencester, Tewkesbury, Bristol, Basingstoke, Rodborough, Stroud, and Hampton Court.

During this one summer, it is estimated that in London and the surrounding counties Whitefield preached to as many as one million people. All London was abuzz with talk about the kingdom of God. Astonishingly, this success occurred while Whitefield was but a mere twenty-four years old. A century later, the Scottish pastor Robert Murray M'Cheyne exclaimed, "O for Whitefield's week in London, when a thousand letters came!"[30] But at the very height of this ministry, Whitefield made a daring decision. Rather than ride this wave of popularity, he determined in August 1739 to board a ship and sail for America. This young evangelist was determined to enter the large cities of the colonies and bring this same evangelistic preaching and revivalist spirit to the New World.

CROSSING THE ATLANTIC

After a two-month voyage, Whitefield landed at Lewes, Delaware, ready to launch a new preaching campaign. This evangelistic tour through the colonies is considered by many the greatest preaching campaign ever undertaken. The influence of Whitefield in America, Martyn Lloyd-Jones said, was "simply overwhelming."[31] A visit by Whitefield, J. I. Packer said, was "a major event."[32] Wherever he went, commerce ceased, shops closed, farmers left their plows, and even judges delayed their hearings. This preaching circuit would set the American landscape ablaze with the truths of the gospel and the need for saving faith in Christ. In due time, a fledgling nation would arise out of the flames.

Whitefield first traveled to Philadelphia, the second-largest city in the colonies, where he preached inside Christ Church and then subsequently moved outdoors. Two days later he addressed upwards of six thousand people, roughly half of the thirteen thousand people who lived in Philadelphia. Whitefield then journeyed to New York City, where he preached to the largest crowds ever gathered in the colonies. He first spoke to eight thousand in a field, then on Sunday to fifteen thousand in the morning, and finally to twenty thousand in the afternoon. Never remaining stationary, he returned to the Philadelphia area, preaching again to swelling numbers in Elizabeth Town, New Brunswick, Maidenhead, and Neshaminy.

On November 24, Whitefield entered Philadelphia with mounting momentum, with multiple thousands attending his preaching. In the mornings, he stood before six thousand people, and in the evenings, eight thousand. The crowds grew to ten thousand, and by Sunday, twenty-five thousand gathered to hear him preach. His farewell address drew upwards of thirty thousand, more than twice the population of the city. Benjamin Franklin, a close friend of Whitefield, documented what he described as "enormous" numbers. Estimating the area covered by the crowd and allowing two square feet for each person, Franklin wrote, "I computed that he might well be heard by more than thirty thousand. This reconciled me to the newspaper accounts of his having preached to twenty-five thousand people in the fields."[33] These vast numbers covered more than a dozen city blocks, and souls were impacted for eternity.

Franklin set out to make Whitefield famous in the colonies. He printed ten editions of Whitefield's *Journals*, and secured the assistance of eleven printers in making them bestsellers. During 1739–1741, more than half the books published by Franklin were by or about Whitefield.[34]

Departing from Philadelphia on November 29, Whitefield journeyed south to Savannah, Georgia, where he preached extensively and tended to his orphanage. In April 1740, he boarded a ship and sailed back north to Lewes; from there he traveled again to Philadelphia and the surrounding areas in order to preach. He rode to New Jersey and New York City, then in May back to Philadelphia, where, on every occasion, he was met with growing success.

Energized by this visible effect, Whitefield boarded a ship again and sailed for Savannah, where he preached numerous times with unusual blessing through the summer. In September he sailed back north, this time to Newport, Rhode Island, where he met with great gospel success. Whitefield pushed north to Boston, preaching for more than a week before advancing up and down the New England coast, heralding Christ in every place. By the time he returned to Boston in October, "The very face of the town seemed to be strangely altered."[35] The power of God was visibly with him wherever he went.

Jonathan Edwards (1703–1758), the recognized leader of the first wave of the Great Awakening, invited Whitefield to Northampton, Massachusetts, where he preached four times in October 1740. This would be the only time that the leaders of this powerful movement would meet. On October 19, Whitefield recorded in his *Journals*, "Preached this morning, and good Mr. Edwards wept during the whole time of exercise. The people were equally affected."[36] Edwards reported that Whitefield's preaching brought "a great alteration in the town."[37] Whitefield and Edwards became the twin instruments God used so mightily during the American Great Awakening. As Perry Miller so aptly put it, "Jonathan Edwards had already put a match to the fuse, and Whitefield blew it into flame."[38]

With no time to waste, in late October and early November Whitefield returned a third time to preach in New York City followed by a fifth time to Philadelphia. He next traveled by land to Savannah, a long and arduous trip of more than a month. There he labored for almost another month. During this excursion, Whitefield preached a total of 175 times within seventy-five days and traveled nearly six thousand miles.[39] He was divinely used as the instrument for rekindling the fires of revival that began several years earlier under the preaching of Jonathan Edwards. Not since New Testament times had the world witnessed such explosive energy and extensive outreach in evangelistic preaching. On January 24, 1741, Whitefield boarded the *Minerva* and departed Savannah for a two-month voyage back to England.

OPPOSITION AND OPPORTUNITIES

Back on British soil, Whitefield was immediately confronted by an unexpected controversy. Having left England at the height of his popularity, he returned a year later to dwindling support. This decline was due to a crisis created by John Wesley over Whitefield's belief in the sovereignty of God in salvation. Before Whitefield's return, Wesley had distributed a tract titled *Free Grace,* a bitter condemnation of the doctrines of grace aimed directly at his old friend. Whitefield responded by defending the biblical teaching of God's election and predestination. However, the damage was done. The painful separation of these spiritual leaders resulted in a division that affected countless people.

Whitefield remained undeterred. Facing mounting attacks in the press and hecklers at his open-air meetings, he persevered in preaching throughout England. He remained undaunted in the face of opposition: "I was honored with having a few stones, dirt, rotten eggs and pieces of dead cats thrown at me."[40] Once, a man tried to take Whitefield's life by attempting to stab him. On other occasions, drummers and trumpeters were hired to drown out his preaching. He was even physically assaulted and beaten: "I received many blows and wounds; one was particularly large, and near my temples. I thought of Stephen. . . . I was in great hopes that like him I should be dispatched, and go off in this bloody triumph to the immediate presence of my Master."[41]

Despite this escalating resistance, Whitefield regained a growing number of supporters. A large building was erected for him in London, Moorfields Tabernacle, in which he could preach whenever he was in the city. John Newton remarked that at five o'clock in the morning, the streets of the Haymarket area in London were as lit with torches carried by the large crowds going to hear Whitefield preach, as they were in the evening with multitudes going to the opera.[42]

Amid his constant travels, Whitefield longed for the companionship of a wife, someone like Jonathan Edwards' Sarah. On November 14, 1741, he hastily married Elizabeth James, a widow he met in Wales whom he barely knew. They had probably spent less than a week together before their marriage. With his new wife at his side, Whitefield preached throughout much of England to swelling numbers and with increased blessing. Next, he undertook a five-month preaching tour of Scotland, which was met with continued success. His sermons, he confessed, came with "much power" accompanied by "very great . . . weeping."[43] The hand of God was upon him for good.

By early 1744, Whitefield was met with financial stress, which demanded his immediate attention. He instructed his wife to leave London with their newly born son, John, and to move into a cottage in Wales in order to reduce their expenses. Traveling in an unheated coach, mother and child stopped halfway in Gloucester, spending a few nights at his parents' Bell Inn. En route, four-month-old John was overtaken by the cold and died. In strange providence, Whitefield's son died in the very home in which George himself had been born, and as he confided, "laid in the church where I was baptized, first communicated, and first preached."[44] As a hammer forges metal upon an anvil, so God used this painful affliction to further shape Whitefield into the image of the suffering Savior whom he was called to preach.

Further difficulty came when Whitefield survived a well-orchestrated assassination plot in which he was attacked while in bed at night. Recognizing God's sovereign protection, he would later say, "We are immortal until our work on earth is done."[45] God still had eternal work for His chosen servant to do, and Whitefield, even in the face of mounting opposition and personal tragedy, would not lose heart.

America again came into his sights, and in 1744, Whitefield embarked upon his third trip to the colonies, accompanied by his wife, her only trip to America. Like a colossal hurricane blowing onto the New England coast, Whitefield made landfall upon spiritually parched ground. This extended ministry would ignite yet another wave of revival. He arrived in critically poor health due to a sickness he had contracted onboard, but proceeded to launch a four-year preaching tour. In failing physical condition, Whitefield sailed to Bermuda in 1748 to recuperate. He preached in Bermuda for two months and quickly recovered, virtually preaching himself back to strength. Later that year, Whitefield returned to Britain in order to dispel reports that he had died in America.

For the next three years (1748–1751), this tireless servant labored throughout England. However, his heart became burdened due to the mounting debts of the Bethesda Orphan House in Georgia. During a time of great financial need, Whitefield providentially came into contact with a wealthy member of England's upper class, Selina Hastings, Countess of Huntingdon, who commissioned him to be her personal chaplain. Lady Huntingdon became a faithful supporter of Whitefield's gospel enterprises and lessened his financial strain. More importantly, this relationship afforded him the opportunity to preach to many British aristocrats at her multiple estates.

Realizing his need to give himself more fully to evangelistic work, Whitefield resigned as the organizational leader of the Calvinistic Methodist Society in 1749. His resignation gave

John Wesley full control of the emerging Evangelical movement and further eased the tension with the Wesley brothers. This allowed Whitefield to preach with greater regularity at his Moorfields Tabernacle in London. Focusing entirely upon his preaching, Whitefield traveled throughout the British Isles, first to Wales, then to Ireland, and finally to Scotland, taking the gospel to more-populated areas.

Whitefield set sail for the New World for the fourth time in October 1751. Undertaking another extensive preaching tour, he first arrived in Georgia to inspect the needs of the Bethesda Orphanage, only to discover its renewed financial shortages, a problem that would follow him for many years. After only six months in the colonies, he was forced to cut short his preaching in order to return to England and raise the much-needed money for his orphan house. Once back in England, Whitefield resumed his extensive preaching. He conducted another ministry tour through Wales and journeyed for a seventh time to Edinburgh. He returned to London for the opening of the newly rebuilt Moorfields Tabernacle, which could house four thousand people. In 1743, yet another tabernacle was built in Bristol to accommodate the large crowds that clamored to hear the great evangelist preach.

A Tireless Itinerant

On a fifth tour of America in 1754, Whitefield again preached throughout the colonies amid rising popularity. This evangelistic tour again stretched from the northern parts of New England to the southern reaches of Georgia. A visit from Whitefield remained a major event, drawing larger crowds than any other preacher. Near Philadelphia, the newly formed College of New Jersey, later named Princeton College, conferred upon him an honorary master of arts degree in recognition of his fundraising efforts on behalf of the school. He returned to Georgia but was stricken with illness because of his weakened state caused by the heavy demands upon him. After only a year in the colonies, Whitefield was forced to return to England in 1755 in order to recover physically.

Whitefield toiled in England for the next eight years due to the French and Indian War, which prevented his return to America. Under a grueling ministry load, he preached throughout the British Isles in places such as Bristol, Gloucester, Edinburgh, Dublin, Glasgow, and Cardiff. Yet with this sustained popularity came increased opposition, which further damaged his already deteriorating health. Nevertheless, with indefatigable resolve, he continued to preach. As revival in England continued, still another tabernacle was built in which Whitefield could preach, the Tottenham Court Road Chapel in central London. He subsequently opened an almshouse for widows in the same area.

In 1759, after more than twenty years, Whitefield was at last able to pay off the debt of the Bethesda Orphan House. Despite the removal of this heavy burden, the frail evangelist was weakening. John Wesley wrote, "Mr. Whitefield . . . seemed to be an old, old man, being fairly worn out in his Master's service."[46] Whitefield's prolific ministry was exacting a high price. Whitefield journeyed to the Netherlands to regain his health. After his health stabilized and the war in America ended, he sailed back to the colonies for a sixth time.

Arriving in Virginia, Whitefield began a two-year preaching tour of the American coast from 1763 to 1765. He initially traveled north to New York, then further upward into New England. He next journeyed south to Georgia, where he preached to large, receptive crowds. He pushed north to Philadelphia, where he was met with further success for the gospel. From there, he departed for England for what would be his final ministry on British soil.

Back in England, Whitefield resumed his heavy preaching load. Based predominantly in London, his ministry knew no rest. He made his final preaching trip to Edinburgh. He faced less persecution wherever he went and was met with greater admiration. Yet he was not without trials. Sorrow came in 1768 when his wife, Elizabeth, unexpectedly died. Despite his grief, his belief in the sovereignty of God remained firm. He preached her funeral sermon from Romans 8:28, affirming that "all things work together for good." He pressed on in his preaching, visiting Trevecca and Wales in extended ministry labors. On September 16, 1769, Whitefield preached his final London sermon from John 10:27–28.

Soon afterward, he sailed for America in what would be his last trip across the Atlantic. This ocean crossing was especially difficult and dangerous, further draining his already depleted strength. Whitefield arrived in Charleston, where he wholeheartedly preached to large crowds for ten consecutive days. He traveled south into Georgia, where he remained for the duration of the winter of 1769–1770. In late spring, he traveled north to launch another extensive evangelistic campaign in Philadelphia, New York, and New England. Under the demands of his constant travel and heavy preaching load, his frail body showed increased signs of deterioration.

Whitefield preached his last sermon in Exeter, New Hampshire, on September 29, 1770. It was a soul-searching exposition that would last two hours, and was titled "Examine Yourself," from 2 Corinthians 13:5. As he stepped forward to preach, Whitefield uttered a silent prayer, "If I have not yet finished my course, let me go and speak for Thee once more in the fields, seal Thy truth, and come home, and die."[47]

Afterward, the drained evangelist rode south by horse to Newburyport, Massachusetts, where he was to preach the next day at the Old South Presbyterian Church. Upon arriving, he addressed a large gathering at the pastor's parsonage on Saturday evening. Having suffered all of his life with severe cardiac asthma, he found it difficult during the night to breathe. On Sunday morning, September 30, 1770, at approximately six o'clock a.m., George Whitefield breathed his last and entered into the presence of Him whom he had so faithfully proclaimed. Biographer Sir Marcus Loane wrote, "At the age of fifty-five, the Prince of English preachers was dead, a prince that hath no peer."[48]

As per his instruction, Whitefield was buried under the next pulpit in which he was to preach. Appropriately, his body was laid in a subterranean crypt under the pulpit of the Old South Presbyterian Church. Multiple funerals were held on both sides of the Atlantic to express sorrow and respect for this gifted servant. The service in Newburyport was attended by six thousand people. So many ships crowded into the harbor that it could contain no more vessels. In London, John Wesley preached Whitefield's memorial service at one of Whitefield's churches, Tottenham Court Road Chapel. There Wesley said:

> Have we read or heard of any person since the Apostles, who testified the Gospel of the grace of God through so widely extended a place, through so large a part of the habitable earth? Have we read or heard of any person who called so many thousands, so many myriads, of sinners to repentance? Above all, have we read or heard of any who has been a blessed instrument in His hand of bringing so many sinners from "darkness to light, and from the power of Satan unto God"?[49]

■ ■ ■

Not quite fifty-six years old at his death, Whitefield had invested thirty-four extraordinary years in the work of advancing the gospel. He had singlehandedly done the work of an entire army of gospel preachers. Even a fraction of Whitefield's evangelistic endeavors would exhaust the strongest of men. From a human perspective, never has one man exerted such far-reaching influence and been met with such enormous success for such an extended period of time as this commanding figure. A century after Whitefield's death, J. C. Ryle remarked:

> No preacher in England has ever succeeded in arresting the attention of such crowds as Whitefield constantly addressed around London. No preacher has ever been so universally popular in every country that he visited, in England, Scotland, and America. No preacher has ever retained his hold on his hearers so entirely as he did for thirty-four years. His popularity never waned.[50]

What uniquely marked this eminently gifted evangelist? In the following chapters, we will examine the evangelistic zeal of this tireless figure.

CHAPTER TWO

A Life of Singular Devotion

Whitefield was the greatest English preacher of all time. . . . His influence in England, his influence in Wales, his influence in Scotland, and his influence in America, in particular, is beyond calculation.[1]

—MARTYN LLOYD-JONES

Any understanding of the evangelistic zeal of George Whitefield must begin with a careful consideration of his personal piety. Even a cursory investigation into his life and ministry reveals a man dominated by a singular devotion to the Lord Jesus Christ. Granted, few spiritual leaders have been endowed with such enormous preaching abilities as this gifted servant. But the reasons for Whitefield's grand success in preaching lay far deeper than his unmatched powers in the pulpit. Greater than his thundering voice was his towering affection for the glory of God. His unparalleled effectiveness

29

as an evangelist cannot be grasped until one sees the depth of his close communion with the Lord.

Observing this Godward passion, J. C. Ryle described Whitefield as "a man of remarkable disinterestedness, and singleness of eye. He seemed to live only for two objects—the glory of God and the salvation of souls."[2] Whitefield's worldwide evangelistic ministry poured forth from his heartfelt pursuit of the glory of God. He was consumed with a fervent desire to know God Himself, which ignited a contagious fire within his soul to lead others to a saving knowledge of Christ.

Whitefield was, as Lloyd-Jones identified, "a pietist, that is, one who saw practical personal devotion to the Father and the Son through the Spirit as always the Christian's top priority."[3] Mark Noll explains, "Pietists are serious about holy living and expend every effort to follow God's law."[4] To this end, Whitefield earnestly prayed, "God give me a deep humility, a well-guided zeal, a burning love and a single eye, and then let men or devils do their worst!"[5]

In his definitive biography of Whitefield, E. A. Johnston noted, "What Whitefield preached he really *believed*. And more than that, what he preached, *he lived*."[6] The message Whitefield proclaimed poured out of a burning and fervent heart for his Master. Simply put, the messenger and his message were one. There was no false dichotomy between his personal life and public ministry, no firewall separating the two. Rather, his preaching contained the burning passions and deep convictions of his own spiritual journey. Out of his heartfelt allegiance to God and Christ, Whitefield rose to proclaim the unsearchable riches of the gospel.

Lloyd-Jones further described Whitefield's life as characterized by "a most amazing piety."[7] This genuine godliness manifested itself throughout Whitefield's personal letters, journal entries, daily encounters, and public proclamation. There should be little doubt as to why God so unusually honored his preaching ministry. Whitefield was able to stand before men because he first kneeled before God.

In this chapter, we will probe into the heart of this remarkable figure and discover the main aspects of his supreme love for Christ. We will give careful consideration to what stoked the blazing fire of his zeal for God. We will note what drove him closer and closer into deeper fellowship with his Lord. The following pages will provide penetrating insight into the depth of Whitefield's intimate communion with the triune God.

IMMERSED IN SCRIPTURE

Whitefield's spiritual devotion was established upon his immovable commitment to the Bible. Once he was converted, the Scripture immediately became his necessary food and fueled the fire in his soul for God. The more he immersed himself in the Bible, the deeper he grew in his dedication to know God and to advance His kingdom. The flame in his soul spread quickly, setting his newly regenerated life ablaze in a relatively short period of time. Within two years, the Word transformed him from a simple student at Oxford into a powerful pulpiteer.[8]

Biographer Arnold Dallimore described Whitefield's early days as a believer, when the only visible light in town would be beaming from his second-story window as he ingested the truths of Holy Writ. Dallimore writes, "We can visualize him at five in the morning in his room over Harris's bookstore. He is on his knees with his Bible, his Greek New Testament, and a volume of Matthew Henry spread before him."[9] With books open before his willing heart, Whitefield gazes back and forth from the English Bible to the Greek to Matthew Henry's commentary, seeking to discern and digest Scripture's divine truths.

Reflecting upon these early days in Christ, Whitefield recalled, "I began to read the Holy Scriptures upon my knees. . . . This proved meat indeed and drink indeed to my soul. I daily received fresh light and power from above."[10] As one who has gone without food devours meat, he described how the Scripture became his "soul's delight."[11] Whitefield confessed how his daily devotion to the Scripture became like fire upon the altar of his soul, fueling his love for Christ.[12]

After reading the text, young Whitefield prayed over "'every line and every word' in both the English and Greek, feasting his mind and his heart upon it till its essential meaning became a part of his very person."[13] Whitefield devoured the words and truths of Scripture like a feast spread before his hungry soul. Little did he realize at the time that God would use his newly kindled heart as a torch whose fire would engulf two continents. As the candle flame flickered in that second-story window, Whitefield was being prepared to be loosed upon the world with the good news of Jesus Christ. His private acquaintance with the Word is most clearly seen in the scriptural vocabulary of his preaching. He readily used biblical metaphors, drew biblical analogies, and illustrated biblical truths with other biblical passages. Cross-references in Scripture flowed freely from his lips as he prayed that the Holy Spirit would sear the truth upon souls in need of divine grace.

The Word of God became so all-consuming in Whitefield's daily life that he confessed to having little time to read anything else: "I got more true knowledge from reading the Book of God in one month, than I could *ever* have acquired from *all* the writings of men."[14] He was deeply troubled by those who viewed the Scripture as an antiquated book of irrelevant writings. In a day when many evangelicals spent considerable time reading secular philosophy, rhetoric, and logic, Whitefield devoured the divine revelation. He grieved over the eclipse of Scripture in his generation, boldly asserting, "If we once get above our Bibles and cease making the written Word of God our sole rule both as to faith and practice, we shall soon lie open to all manner of delusion and be in great danger of making shipwreck of faith and a good conscience."[15] Whitefield resolved that nothing would displace the preeminence of Scripture in his life.

As Whitefield lived for Christ, the Word of God became the ruling authority over his life. It marked the trail upon which he constantly discovered beautiful vistas of redemption, sacrifice, love, and joy. The Scripture caused him to love God yet more. "Study to know Him more and more, for the more you know, the more you will love Him,"[16] he said. Whitefield desired to become more like his Lord with every word he read, and he was forged and formed upon the anvil of Scripture. His great devotion to Scripture became God's descending communion with him.

SATURATED WITH PRAYER

Moreover, Whitefield was devoted to God in earnest prayer. Through time spent on his knees, his heart for God was further deepened and developed. The real secret of his public ministry was not found primarily in his vivid vocabulary, dramatic skills, or Oxford education. The true source of power in his preaching lay far deeper. It was discovered behind closed doors in time alone with God. He urged, "Be much in secret prayer. Converse less with man, and more with God."[17] Whitefield poured out his heart to God in prayer, and he was effectively used before men.

Biographer Robert Philip identified Whitefield's prayer life as a main source of his spiritual success: "The grand secret of Whitefield's power was, as we have seen and felt, his *devotional* spirit. Had he been less prayerful, he would have been less powerful."[18] Whitefield was much *for* God because he was much *with* Him. From the moment Christ dawned in his heart, Whitefield was absorbed in intimate prayer. He knew a servant could not fulfill his assignment without a regular audience with his Master. As a new convert he remarked, "I would be so overpowered with a sense of God's Infinite Majesty that I would be compelled to throw myself on the ground and offer my soul as a blank in his hands, to write on it what he pleased."[19] Like Isaiah, Ezekiel, or John, who found themselves prostrate before the infinite majesty of God, Whitefield knew he would be useful in God's kingdom to the extent that he assumed such a lowly posture.

Far from viewing prayer as empty drudgery, Whitefield saw it as sheer delight. It was a private encounter with God. With the veil drawn back from the Holy of Holies, he entered in order to fellowship with his Father. Recounting one particular season in prayer, he said, "Oh, what sweet communion had I daily vouchsafed with God in prayer. . . . How often have I been carried out beyond myself when sweetly meditating in the fields! How assuredly have I felt that Christ dwelt in me and I in Him!"[20] In reality, the entire world was his prayer closet, wherever his preaching took him. Whether aboard a ship, riding on horseback through fields, or standing atop a wooden barrel for a pulpit, Whitefield maintained constant contact with the throne of grace.

Whitefield understood that prayer was a necessary spiritual discipline for the grounding and growth of his soul. Whitefield's diary begins with a list of criteria he regularly used as a basis of examining himself and his actions. This list is as follows:

Have I,

1. Been fervent in private prayer?
2. Used stated hours of prayer?
3. Used prayer every hour?
4. After or before every deliberate conversation or action, considered how it might tend to God's glory?
5. After any pleasure, immediately given thanks?
6. Planned business for the day?
7. Been simple and recollected in everything?
8. Been zealous in undertaking and active in doing what good I could?
9. Been meek, cheerful, affable in everything I said or did?
10. Been proud, vain, unchaste, or enviable of others?
11. Recollected in eating and drinking? Thankful? Temperate in sleep?
12. Taken time for giving thanks according to [William] Law's rules?
13. Been diligent in studies?
14. Thought or spoken unkindly of anyone?
15. Confessed all sins?[21]

Prayer is mentioned in six of these fifteen maxims, more than any other spiritual discipline. Here, the importance Whitefield placed upon prayer can be clearly seen. He saw time alone with God as the catalyst that brings "God and man together." He explained, "It raises man up to God, and brings God down to man."[22] Consequently, he spent prolonged seasons in prayer: "Once we spent a whole night in prayer and praise; and many a time, at midnight and at one in the morning, after I have been wearied almost to death in preaching, writing and conversation, and going from place to place, God imparted new life to my soul, and enabled me to intercede with Him for an hour and a half and two hours together."[23] Whitefield viewed prayer as a fountain of refreshing water for his parched soul. The more he prayed, the more powerfully he preached and the more sinners were converted to Christ.

To this end, Whitefield exhorted others, "Be much in secret, set prayer. When you are about the common business of life, be much in prayer."[24] He was insistent that our infinite God is acutely aware of the pleas of even the poorest and weariest souls. Whitefield testified, "He is a prayer-hearing God"[25] and believed that prayer "is one of the most noble parts of the believer's spiritual armour."[26] His firm confidence in God who heard his prayers brought him, repeatedly, into the inner sanctum where the angels continually cry, "Holy, holy, holy." Herein lies the true source of power behind such mighty preaching.

FOCUSED ON CHRIST

Further, Whitefield's devotion meant he maintained a singular focus upon Jesus Christ. There can be no understanding of what drove Whitefield apart from recognizing his fixed gaze upon Christ. Lloyd-Jones remarked, "No man ever knew more of the love of Christ than this man. It sometimes overwhelmed him and almost crushed him physically. He would be bathed in tears because of it."[27] This intense focus upon Christ was the dominant note of his extraordinary life and ministry. Concerning his myopic gaze upon the Lord, Whitefield insisted, "One thing is needful."[28] Jesus Christ was everything—his Master, message, and motivation.

Stephen Mansfield described this obsessive fixation that Whitefield had with his Savior when he wrote:

> His one true love was always the person of Jesus. The risen Christ was the fixed star of his life's voyage, the sole object of his affections. It was for Jesus for whom he lived, Jesus whom he sought to please, and Jesus in whom he hoped to find his rest. . . . Indeed, as Whitefield understood, passion for Jesus is the personal renewal from which greater revivals spring.[29]

The magnifying lens through which Whitefield saw Christ was Scripture. He maintained, "Look, therefore, always for Christ in the Scripture. He is the treasure hid in the field, both of the Old and New Testaments. In the Old you will find Him under prophecies, types, sacrifices, and shadows; in the New, manifested in the flesh, to become a propitiation for our sins as a priest, and as a prophet to reveal the whole will of his heavenly Father."[30] Every stone in Scripture, he believed, must be overturned in search of Christ.

The Old Testament served as a dark glass through which Whitefield beheld Christ in part, while the New Testament reveals Him in His fullness. Whitefield implored his listeners to always keep Christ in view when studying the Scriptures and to use each verse as a vehicle to bring them closer to the Messiah.[31] He was convinced that the written Word should always lead to a deeper experience of the living Word, Jesus Christ.

Above all, Whitefield's desire was to know Jesus Christ. He stated, "We can preach the Gospel of Christ no further than we have experienced the power of it in our own hearts."[32] Since Christ is the core of the gospel, Whitefield believed he must have a strong devotion to Him in order to be effective in preaching Him. A preacher will proclaim Christ in demonstration of power as he is personally acquainted with Him. He wanted a "felt Christ." By this, Whitefield meant that he must have an experiential knowledge of Christ by which he would grow closer in his personal walk with the Lord. Countless eyewitnesses testified of being fearful during his preaching because of the solemn realization that they had been in the presence of Christ.

Therefore, Whitefield encouraged his hearers to "live near to Christ. . . . Hunger and thirst daily after the righteousness of Christ."[33] There could be no substitute, no shortcut, no detour in this spiritual journey to Christlikeness. He asserted, "I wish all names among the saints of God were swallowed up in that one word *Christian.* I long for professors to leave off placing religion in saying, 'I am a Churchman,' 'I am a Dissenter.' My language to such is, 'Are you of Christ? If so, I love you with all my heart.'"[34]

Is it any wonder that Whitefield's preaching was continually pointing people to Jesus Christ? His focus must be their focus, which necessitated that they be looking to Christ.

CLOAKED IN HUMILITY

In addition, Whitefield's piety was evidenced in his remarkable humility. No one can read about this gifted evangelist's life without being impressed by his modesty. Throughout his ministry, Whitefield never lost sight of the fact that he was a wretched sinner saved by grace. He was, in the words of Lloyd-Jones, "a most humble man."[35] J. C. Ryle adds, "Certainly, there was no more humble man."[36] Still, Whitefield repeatedly confessed, "I am less than the least of all saints, I am the chief of sinners."[37] He viewed himself as "less than the least of all."[38] Despite attaining celebrity status, this preeminent evangelist remained possessed with a lowly state of mind.

John Gillies, an early biographer of Whitefield, noted that he possessed "the deepest humility and self-abasement."[39] This gifted preacher would not allow a Christian institution to be named after him. Neither would he allow any movement to bear his name. He never sought the limelight or applause. To the contrary, Whitefield pursued the honor of Jesus Christ in the salvation of lost souls. He never forgot that he was a mere servant enlisted into the service of his Master. This sober realization created within him a "humble, thankful, and resigned heart."[40] Another Whitefield biographer, Arnold Dallimore, concurred, "He turned from the place of prominence and became as he said, 'simply the servant of all.'"[41] Concerning such modesty, Ryle agreed, "Again and again, in the very zenith of his popularity, we find him speaking of himself and his works in the lowliest of terms."[42]

Whitefield knew a self-absorbed life would cripple his evangelistic efforts. He understood that any self-obsession would render him ineffective for God's wider purposes. After self-examination he lamented, "O this self-love, this self-will! It is the devil of devils. Lord Jesus, may thy blessed Spirit purge it out of all our hearts!"[43] As he gazed inward, he observed his own heart, prone to pride, self-love, and "all manner of corruption."[44] The more he looked upon Christ's holiness, the more he became aware of his own sin. This self-awareness of his own spiritual poverty drove him to confess the corruption in his heart. Like a brush upon a canvas sweeping back and forth until the predetermined portrait emerges, Whitefield saw self-denial as the sanctifying motion upon his heart, creating a masterpiece of Christ-like humility.

Such meekness was further evidenced in Whitefield's teachable spirit. He was willing to concede the error of his ways whenever he discovered he was wrong. He confessed, "Whatever errors I have been, or shall be guilty of in my ministry, I hope the Lord will show me, and give me grace to amend."[45] For example, after reviewing his published *Journals,* he concluded that he had unfairly criticized others. To correct this wrong, he edited a new edition, acknowledging: "In my former *Journal,* taking things by hearsay too much, I spoke and wrote too rashly, both of the colleges and ministers of New England; for which as I have already done, when at Boston last, from the pulpit, I take this opportunity of asking public pardon from the press. It was rash and uncharitable, and, though well meant, I fear did hurt."[46] Of these wrongs, Whitefield repented publicly and asked for forgiveness from all offended parties:

> In how many things have I judged and acted wrong. I have been too rash and hasty in giving characters, both of places and persons. Being fond of scripture language, I have often used a style too apostolical, and at the same time I have been too bitter in my zeal. Wild-fire has been mixed with it, and I find that I frequently wrote and spoke in my own spirit, when I thought I was writing and speaking by the assistance of the Spirit of God.[47]

This self-abasing meekness was also seen in the salutations he wrote at the end of his letters. He would often sign: "Your unworthy friend, brother, and servant in our dear Lord's vineyard,"[48] "Your very humble servant, in our dear Lord Jesus,"[49] or, "Your most affectionate, though unworthy brother."[50] Such self-denial was also heard from his lips, as he repeatedly exclaimed, "Let the name of George Whitefield perish so long as Christ is exalted."[51] It was never his desire to have the name *Whitefield* exalted. The more he beheld Christ, the more he realized Christ must increase, and he must decrease (John 3:30).

But perhaps the supreme example of Whitefield's humility concerned his theological differences and strained relationships with the Wesley brothers. For the sake of peace, he chose to resign his leadership role in the Methodist movement, which he had helped to start. He assumed a lesser place, even to the point of appearing as John Wesley's "assistant." A self-deprecating man, Whitefield was willing to submit to those outside his own theological convictions.[52] The inner heart cry of Whitefield remained, "God, give me a deep humility."[53] This was a prayer that God chose to answer. As Whitefield humbled himself before God, he became the chief catalyst in launching the trans-Atlantic revivals of the eighteenth century.

STRIVING FOR HOLINESS

Finally, Whitefield's godliness was witnessed in his constant pursuit of personal holiness. As he read the Bible and communed with God, he grew spiritually as the divine work of sanctification was being performed in him. His self-abasing spirit exposed his sin and gave a keen awareness of his need for moral purity. Holiness was the goal of his spiritual disciplines. J. C. Ryle noted that of all the preachers of the eighteenth century, Whitefield was "one of its most saintly characters, if not the saintliest of all."[54] So godly was he, there was never a legitimate scandal that surrounded his personal life. He remained free from any accusation that could be raised against his inward character or outward conduct.

In the midst of his demanding ministry, Whitefield urged others to intercede for his advance in godliness. He implored his followers, "Let none of my friends cry to such a sluggish, lukewarm, unprofitable worm, 'Spare thyself.' Rather spur me on, I pray you, with an 'Awake, thou sleeper, and begin to do something for thy God.'"[55] No matter how dedicated he was to God, he was convinced he must be more so, regardless of the personal price he must pay. The more he recognized his need for greater holiness, the more he entreated his supporters to pray for this growth in grace.

For his holiness to deepen, Whitefield understood that he must be continuously turning away from sin. He defined such repentance as "hatred of sin." He claimed, "It is not just confessing yourselves to be sinners, it is not knowing your condition to be sad and deplorable, so long as you continue in your sins; your care and endeavours should be, to get the heart thoroughly affected, therewith, that you may feel yourselves to be lost and undone creatures. . . . Resolve to leave all thy sinful lusts and pleasures."[56] Holiness cannot be obtained, he maintained, as long as one clings to sin. Whitefield, therefore, knew that he must be constantly striving to separate himself from sin.

Whitefield contended that repentance breaks the dam of sin, which withholds the fullness of God's grace from flowing into his life. He declared, "Abhor thy old sinful course of life, and serve God in holiness and righteousness all the remaining part of life. If you lament and bewail past sins, and do not forsake them, your repentance is in vain, you are mocking of God, and deceiving your own soul; you must put off the old man with his deeds, before you can put on the new man, Christ Jesus."[57] Whitefield's own repentance would transform his heart from being lifeless and lukewarm to being vibrant and fervent for God. If he was to preach with power, Whitefield knew such integrity and purity must be present within him.

Throughout his Christian walk, Whitefield recognized holiness as a progressive transformation from one degree of glory to another (2 Cor. 3:18). Moral perfection, he contended, was not ultimately attainable until he entered the heavenly realm. This understanding was diametrically opposed to the perfectionism taught by the Wesleys, who asserted that a believer could cease sinning. Whitefield countered that perfect holiness could never be fully realized upon this earth. His sanctification was a continual process, realized through the spiritual disciplines of Bible study and prayer. These pursuits, in turn, produced humility and holiness within him.

From the effectual calling of the Spirit in salvation to

his final breath upon this earth, Whitefield diligently sought personal holiness throughout his life and ministry. Is it any wonder that God chose to use such a holy vessel in the preaching of His Word?

. . .

Throughout the centuries, few Christian leaders have displayed greater spirituality as did this "Grand Itinerant." As we peel back the layers of George Whitefield and peer into his soul, we discover the true source of his spiritual power. Behind his revivalistic preaching was a burning zeal for the Lord. The embers of his intense spirit glowed red hot for God, resulting in a preaching ministry that was energized with supernatural power.

Such heart devotion to God dominated Whitefield's life. This remarkable passion for godliness animated his preaching, in unprecedented fashion, on both sides of the Atlantic. Baring his soul, he repeatedly presented himself to God as a living and holy sacrifice:

> I give to Him my soul and body to be disposed and worn out in His labours as He shall think meet. I do hence resolve, by His assistance . . . to lead a stricter life than ever, to give my self to prayer and the study of the Scriptures. . . . God give me my health, if it be His blessed will . . . I give myself wholly to Him.[58]

This was the heart cry of a man wholly given to God. The depth of Whitefield's spirituality made room for the broad expanse of his preaching of the gospel. He stated: "I always observed, as my inward strength increased, so my outward sphere of action increased proportionately."[59] This direct corollary between his personal spirituality and his public ministry must be acknowledged. In the chapters ahead, we will note how this inward piety of Whitefield informed his preaching, with history-altering effects.

May Whitefield serve as an example to a new generation of soldiers in the army of Christ to become more immersed in Scripture, saturated with prayer, focused on Christ, cloaked in humility, and striving for holiness. May God give His church such sanctified servants.

CHAPTER THREE

A Theology of Sovereign Grace

Whitefield possessed a very real understanding of the doctrines of grace, not as an abstract system of thought, but as the teachings of the Scriptures and as the basic principles of his daily Christian life.[1]

—ARNOLD DALLIMORE

George Whitefield was arguably the most prolific evangelist since the time of the Apostles. Yet, at the same time, he was also a staunch Calvinist. Undergirding his passionate gospel preaching was an unwavering belief in God's sovereignty in man's salvation. It was the doctrines of grace that ignited his soul with holy compulsion to reach the world with the message of Christ. Some argue that these two realities—sovereign grace and evangelistic zeal—cannot co-exist. But nothing could be further from the truth. They meet perfectly in Scripture, and they existed side-by-side in Whitefield's ministry. No preaching can be any stronger than the doctrine upon which it is based, and the truths of sovereign grace proved to be the sturdy foundation in the ministry of this prolific evangelist.

Whitefield possessed, according to J. I. Packer, a "classic Augustinian frame of sovereign grace."[2] Historian Lee Gatiss, a compiler of Whitefield's sermons, wrote that he was "a firm believer in the Reformed doctrine of salvation and Reformed biblical theology."[3] Another church historian, Mark Noll, concurred: "He preached on the bound will, the electing power of God, and the definite atonement—all themes of traditional Calvinism."[4] Though a strict Calvinist, Whitefield nevertheless derived his theological convictions, not from reading John Calvin, but from studying Scripture itself. The hours he spent poring over the Word led him to passionately embrace the clear teaching of sovereign grace in Scripture.

"I embrace the Calvinistic scheme, not because of Calvin, but Jesus Christ has taught it to me,"[5] Whitefield said. In fact, he rarely mentioned Calvin in his letters or sermons. Rather, he relied, first and foremost, upon the plain testimony of Scripture. In an early letter to John Wesley in 1740, Whitefield wrote, "Alas, I never read anything that Calvin wrote; my doctrines I have from Christ and His apostles; I was taught them of God."[6] Whitefield read and studied God's Word, and from it drew these deep convictions—the very same core beliefs that Calvin also upheld.

According to E. A Johnston, "To understand George Whitefield and what made him tick, we need to know his theology."[7] Further, "It is the *motive* which *moved* him. . . . The doctrines of grace gave him fire in the pulpit to cry out and warn men of the wrath to come and to flee from it into the loving arms of a wonderful Savior."[8] The theological convictions of Whitefield emboldened him in all that he practiced and proclaimed. From the beginning of his ministry, his adherence to the doctrines of grace laid the cornerstone upon which he built his entire ministry.

Contrary to the popular Calvinistic stereotype, Whitefield was not a stale, stoic intellectual with a dour approach to Christianity. He was fervently enlivened by the sovereign grace of God, which sparked an intense urgency in his gospel preaching. It was his belief in the doctrines of grace that propelled his gospel proclamation far and wide. The deeper Whitefield plunged into these sacred truths, the higher he ascended in his declaration of them. Writing to Howell Harris, a leader in the Welsh revival, Whitefield spoke of the need to preach God's free, electing grace to his listeners, especially to the unconverted:

> Put them in mind of the freeness and eternity of God's electing love, and be instant with them to lay hold of the perfect righteousness of Jesus Christ by faith. Talk to them, oh talk to them till midnight, of the riches of His all-sufficient grace. Tell them, oh tell them, what He has done for their souls, and how earnestly He is now interceding for them in heaven. . . . Press on

them to believe immediately! Intersperse prayers with your exhortations, and thereby call down fire from heaven, even the fire of the Holy Ghost. . . . Speak every time, my dear brother, as if it were your last. Weep out, if possible, every argument, and as it were, compel them to cry, "behold how He loveth us!"[9]

Standing in strictest solidarity with the Reformers and Puritans, Whitefield asserted, "You know how strongly I assert all the doctrines of grace, as held forth in the Westminster Confession of Faith and the doctrinal articles of the Church of England. These I trust I shall adhere to as long as I live because I verily believe they are the truths of God, and have felt the power of them in my own heart."[10] In this, we see that Whitefield's preaching was firmly rooted and grounded in the absolute supremacy of God in the salvation of fallen sinners. It was these towering truths, sometimes identified as the five points of Calvinism, that ignited his soul and empowered his history-altering preaching on two continents. To remove the doctrines of sovereign grace from Whitefield's life and ministry would have been to extinguish the very fire in his bones.

In the centuries before Whitefield, Calvinistic theology dominated the landscape of English Christianity, from the reign of Elizabeth I until the end of the Commonwealth. However, by the eighteenth century, Reformed doctrine was in sharp decline. J. I. Packer explained, "Following the

Restoration, many Anglican minds, recoiling from all things Calvinistic, took up with a moralistic, indeed legalistic, recasting of justification by faith."[11] Even the new colonies were already suffering from the plague of Arminianism and antinomianism. Harvard University, once a bastion of Calvinistic truth, had already succumbed to these debilitating, man-centered doctrines.

Whitefield is to be credited with assuming a leading role in the Calvinistic resurgence on both sides of the Atlantic. Instead of retreating into the shadows of a lifeless Christianity, Whitefield boldly promoted biblical Calvinism, which produces sound conversions, genuine revival, and authentic godliness. He maintained, "These are the doctrines which, when attended with a divine energy, and preached with power, always have, and always will . . . make their way through the world, however weak the instrument that delivers them may be."[12] Calvinism, Whitefield asserted, is that truth which propels God's work in the world, wherever it is proclaimed.

In this chapter, we will consider Whitefield's commitment to each of the five doctrines of grace. Whitefield drank deeply from the well of the doctrines of grace, and it proved to be the spring of all he believed and preached. Each tenet of Calvinism shaped and molded him into a zealous evangelist. When Whitefield stood to preach, he was gripped with an enormous confidence in God, believing His eternal purposes were moving forward with unalterable certainty.

TOTAL DEPRAVITY

Whitefield held to the biblical doctrine of total depravity. This is the scriptural teaching that the original sin of Adam was imputed to the entire human race, condemning all subsequent generations. Likewise, the sin nature of Adam was transmitted to every person at the moment of their conception. Every faculty of every person—mind, affections, and will—is fatally plagued by sin. The entire fallen race cannot, by its own moral efforts, save itself. Neither does any sinful creature have faith to believe in Christ. Whitefield believed that man is utterly dead in sin, and his will is held captive in bondage.

R. Elliot, a prominent minister converted under White-field's early ministry, outlined the great evangelist's theological stance on total depravity: "He taught the Scripture doctrine of original sin, which consists in these two things: First, Adam's personal offense imputed; and, second, the entire depravity of his fallen nature, imparted to all his seed."[13] Whitefield insisted upon the imputation of Adam's sin to the entire human race: "By original sin I mean nothing less than the imputation of Adam's first sin to all his posterity by ordinary generation . . . the consequence of which is, that inherent corruption of nature, and those sinful propensities, we are now born with into the world."[14] Whitefield considered this truth to be so important that he called original sin "the very foundation of the Christian religion."[15] He further affirmed that it "can never be denied by anyone who believes that St. Paul's epistles were written by divine inspiration; where we are told that 'in Adam all died,' that is, Adam's sin was imputed to all."[16] Precisely as Scripture teaches, Whitefield believed all people are, by nature, "sinners and children of wrath."[17]

Whitefield maintained that original sin leaves the human race spiritually dead. Sinful man is morally incapable of eradicating himself of the sin that clings so tightly to his fallen nature. Man is radically depraved and unable to raise himself from the ash heap of his fallenness. To deny this biblical teaching, Whitefield held, "is nothing but a want of being well grounded"[18] in Scripture. Those who refuse this truth may "call themselves Christians,"[19] he said, but they are "so very lukewarm in their love and affections to Jesus Christ."[20] Whitefield believed that man rejects the teachings of original sin and total depravity due to inherent pride. Man does not like to be painted in such black colors or to be told he is incapable of lifting himself up if he so chooses.[21]

By their fallen nature, sinners rebel against the truth of original sin, Whitefield said, because they "obstinately shut their eyes against the light of the glorious gospel of Christ."[22] He explained:

That little children are guilty, I mean, that they are conceived and born in sin, is plain from the whole tenor of the Book of God. David was a man after God's own heart, yet, says he, "I was conceived in sin." Jeremiah, speaking of everyone's heart, says "The heart of man is deceitful and desperately wicked above

55

all things." God's servants unanimously declare (and Paul cites it from one of them) that "we are altogether now become abominable, altogether gone out of the way of original righteousness, there is not one of us that doeth good (by nature), no not one."[23]

Whitefield's understanding of total depravity indelibly marked his preaching. Virtually every sermon Whitefield preached pointed man to his desperate condition in sin. He confronted his unconverted listeners: "You are in a state of damnation. . . . I tell thee, O man; I tell thee, O woman, whoever thou art, thou art a dead man, thou art a dead woman, nay a damned man, a damned woman, without a new heart."[24] He preached that man must acknowledge his utter helplessness before he can recognize the need to embrace Christ as his only hope.

Whitefield boldly pressed this truth upon his hearers. He reiterated that fallen man is born spiritually dead, estranged from Christ, and under the judgment and wrath of almighty God. "I affirm that we all stand in need of being justified, on account of the sin of our natures: for we are all chargeable with original sin, or the sin of our first parents,"[25] he maintained. This sobering doctrine of total depravity loomed large within the theological framework of George Whitefield.

UNCONDITIONAL ELECTION

Whitefield likewise embraced the biblical doctrine of sovereign election. He maintained that before time began, God the Father freely chose those whom He would save out of the whole of the fallen race. These chosen ones were elected not on the basis of anything good foreseen in them, and certainly not for any foreseen faith in Christ. God chose to set His sovereign love upon certain individuals for reasons known only to Himself. Whitefield speaks of this truth as "a doctrine whereby God is eminently glorified and His people greatly edified and comforted."[26] He believed God has chosen a people by Himself and for Himself who are predestined to be saved by Christ.

Whitefield firmly held to the Reformed position on predestination. In this biblical view, from all eternity God decrees some to election and intervenes in their lives to work regeneration and faith by a divine act of grace, bringing them all to Himself in eternity future. Whitefield saw election as "the fountain from which all blessings flow."[27] He maintained that election "shines with such resplendent brightness that all the blessings they [believers] receive, all the privileges they do or will enjoy, through Jesus Christ, flow from the everlasting love of God the Father."[28]

In a sermon titled "The Good Shepherd," Whitefield preached, "We are His by eternal election: *the sheep which Thou hast give Me,* says Christ. They were given by God the Father to Christ Jesus, in the covenant made between the Father and the Son from all eternity."[29] Whitefield believed of this eternal contract, "that if He would obey and suffer, and make Himself a sacrifice for sin, He should see His seed, He should prolong His days, and the pleasure of the Lord should prosper in His hands."[30] This covenant is so immutably fixed in eternity past that all individuals elected by the Father to salvation were given to the Son to be His possession, never to be cast away.

In Whitefield's day, as in ours, the doctrine of unconditional election remained a doctrine of disdain. However, Whitefield viewed this teaching with sheer delight and pleasure, seeing within it the shining of the glory of God. Rather than seeing it as an irrelevant detail, Whitefield believed election is a life-altering truth that produces humility: "I cannot see how true humbleness of mind can be attained without a knowledge of it; and though I will not say, that every one who denies election is a bad man, yet I will say . . . it is a very bad sign . . . for, if we deny election, we must, partly at least, glory in ourselves."[31] Those who do not adhere to this precious truth risk finding themselves in the dangerous bog of self-love and self-glory. Yet, Whitefield asserted, the one who embraces unconditional election relishes the glory of his sovereign Redeemer.

Whitefield was also convinced that the doctrine of election has great converting power. Far from seeing election as a stumbling block to evangelism, he said, "The Scriptural doctrine of election and predestination as we believe and preach it is no discouragement to sinners, no bar to any one's conversion: for our warrant to come to Christ, is not God's secret decree and purpose concerning us; but His inviting, calling and commanding us in His Word to repent and believe on Christ."[32]

Whitefield certainly rejected the excuse "I cannot come to Christ and be saved, because I am not one of the elect." God's election, he affirmed, does not negate man's responsibility to hear the countless invitations in Scripture to come and believe in Christ. Quite the contrary, sinners find great confidence in unconditional election because the one who believes and comes to Christ is found among God's chosen ones.

God withholds from the non-elect this work of saving grace, passing them by and leaving them to themselves, a biblical truth known as reprobation. In an extended letter to John Wesley from Bethesda, Georgia, on December 24, 1740, Whitefield wrote, "Without doubt, the doctrine of election and reprobation must stand or fall together. . . . I believe the doctrine of reprobation, that God intends to give saving grace, through Jesus Christ, only to a certain number; and that the rest of mankind, after the fall of Adam, being justly left of God to continue in sin, will at last suffer that eternal death which is its proper wages."[33]

DEFINITE ATONEMENT

Whitefield also championed the doctrine of definite atonement, also known as particular redemption. Lee Gatiss wrote, "Whitefield gloried in . . . particular redemption, or as it is sometimes known, definite or 'limited atonement.' This is the teaching that the Father's election, the Son's redemption, and the Spirit's application of salvation are all coextensive;

that God planned to save a certain people, His sheep . . . and sent His Son explicitly to achieve this goal."[34] God the Father designed the death of the Lord Jesus Christ with the specific purpose of saving His elect. Christ laid down His life for those whom the Father had given Him in eternity past. Simply put, Jesus died for His sheep, the chosen bride of Christ.

Definite atonement was an essential element in Whitefield's explanation of the gospel. Whitefield declared, "There was an eternal compact between the Father and Son. A certain number was then given Him, as the purchase and reward of His obedience and death. For these He prayed, and not for this world. For these and these only, He is now interceding, and with their salvation, He will be fully satisfied."[35] His preaching flourished with such references to the eternal purpose of Christ's death. In describing the cross, Whitefield proclaimed, "[Christ] was about to offer up His soul an offering for the sins of the elect."[36] Whitefield believed the extent of Christ's death did not include the whole world, but only those whom the Father had chosen out of the world.

This remained Whitefield's firm conviction to the end. In what would be his final sermon delivered on English soil, the great evangelist stated, "Christ purchased those whom He calls His own; He redeemed them with His own blood, so that they are not only His by eternal election, but also by actual redemption."[37] Whitefield grasped the indivisible union between sovereign election and particular redemption, a core belief he upheld throughout the entirety of his preaching ministry.

Conversely, Whitefield warned against a belief in a universal atonement, which inevitably leads to belief in the libertarian free will of man. He held that these two positions—universal redemption and free will—are inseparably bound together: "If universal redemption, taken in a literal sense, be admitted, the equally unscriptural notions of universal salvation, or justification by works, and salvation by man's free will, together with that of the possibility of falling away from a state of grace, totally and finally, must unavoidably follow."[38] Whitefield insisted that preaching universal redemption causes a lost world to be hypnotized into a false sense of security and lulled into an unwarranted peace.

Many argue that definite atonement drains the energy out of evangelism. They contend that it makes gospel preaching meaningless. But a cursory examination of Whitefield's sermons reveals the opposite. It is a false assumption to presume one cannot believe in the definite atonement of Christ and be a passionate gospel evangelist. Far from undermining his evangelism, particular redemption stoked the flames of Whitefield's evangelistic zeal.[39] He asserted, "[Christ] knows every one for whom He died; and if there were to be one missing for whom Christ died, God the Father would send Him down again from heaven to fetch him."[40] Whitefield freely offered the glorious good news of the cross of Christ as a sufficient sacrifice for all who would believe.

Such an unwavering belief did not annul Whitefield's sense of responsibility to proclaim the gospel to everyone without discrimination. We can almost see his cheeks streaming with tears and hear his dramatic voice pleading with the throngs to come to Christ. In his sermon on the conversion of Zaccheus, Whitefield exclaimed:

> There, there, by faith, O mourners in Zion, may you see your Savior hanging with arms stretched out, and hear Him, as it were, thus speaking to your souls; "Behold how I have loved you! Behold My hands and My feet! Look, look into My wounded side, and see a heart flaming with love; love stronger than death. Come into My arms, O sinners, come wash your spotted souls in My heart's blood."[41]

Unquestionably, George Whitefield presented the atoning sacrifice of Christ as applicable to all who would come to Him for salvation.

EFFICACIOUS CALL

Whitefield further preached that all those chosen by the Father and redeemed by the Son would be regenerated by the Holy Spirit. The saving work of Christ on the cross is applied by the effectual call of the Holy Spirit. He held that the third person of the Trinity would convict the elect sinner, efficaciously draw him to Christ, and grant the gifts of true repentance and faith.

As Whitefield preached the gospel, he believed certain listeners would be divinely enabled to respond to the gospel call. He maintained that "they must be regenerated, they must be born again, they must be renewed in the very spirit, in the inmost faculties of their minds, before they can truly call Christ, 'Lord, Lord.'"[42] Whitefield believed that regeneration is monergistic, an exclusive work of God in the human heart that both precedes and produces saving faith. When God exercises this sovereign grace in the human soul, Whitefield understood, the Spirit always secures the effect that He intends.

According to R. Elliot, Whitefield believed "man has no power or will at all to effect his own conversion, it being the entire work of God's Spirit."[43] Since man is born spiritually dead, there is absolutely nothing he can do to bring salvation to his soul, independent of the Spirit. The will of every man is imprisoned in sin and bound by Satan, and cannot break free unless the Holy Spirit liberates him to believe in Christ. Therefore, the beginning, middle, and end of the new birth are entirely the work of the triune God, for which He is to receive all honor and glory in salvation.

Elliot continued, "Whitefield also very consistently maintained that the grace of God in the conversion of a sinner is irresistible; and indeed he who denies it cannot truly believe that man is entirely fallen."[44] As Whitefield preached to the unconverted masses, he acknowledged that the Spirit must cause sinners to believe: "O that He may call you by His Spirit, and make you a willing people in this day of His power! For I know my calling will not do, unless He, by His efficacious grace, compel you to come in."[45] Whitefield was not saying that man cannot resist the outward call to come to Christ in salvation. The history of the world is filled with the story of man's opposition to the call of the gospel. But he nevertheless believed that God by His inward call can overcome such resistance within the heart of the elect. The Spirit must open their ears to the Savior's effectual call to faith.

Knowing that no sinner can cause his own regeneration, Whitefield would urge the unconverted to pray that God would give them a new heart and the faith to believe: "O that I could see some of you sensible of this, and hear you cry out, 'Lord, break this hard heart; Lord, deliver me from the body of this death; draw me, Lord, make me willing to come after Thee; I am lost; Lord, save me, or I perish!'"[46] He asserted that unbelieving sinners must ask God to make them willing to believe in Christ.

Likening the unregenerate man to the lifeless state of a corpse, Whitefield declared, "The sinner can no more raise himself from the deadness of sin than Lazarus, who had been dead four days, until Jesus came and cried out, 'Lazarus, come forth.'"[47] When the Holy Spirit calls sinners to come forth from the dead, they are made new creatures in Christ. Resurrected from their fallen state, their hearts of stone are supernaturally re-created as hearts of flesh.

PRESERVING GRACE

Finally, Whitefield upheld the biblical doctrine of the perseverance of the saints. The work of sovereign grace does not end at conversion. What God in the corridors of eternity past had predestined to take place, He will bring to completion in eternity future. Whitefield was convinced that God brings all His chosen ones to future glory. Those whom God elects and brings to salvation will be preserved by grace, both in time and eternity. Those whom God saves, He saves forever. They will never fall away. They will never perish.

Elliot articulated Whitefield's position on this doctrine of preserving grace: "He taught and maintained the final perseverance of the saints: not indeed by the power of their own free will, nor by virtue of their own faithfulness, but by the power and faithfulness of God; for whom He justified, them He also glorified, Romans 8:30."[48] This final link in the golden chain of salvation ensures the eternal security of all elect believers.

This doctrine brought great joy to Whitefield throughout his Christian life and ministry. In addressing John 10:28—"I give unto them eternal life; and they shall never perish, neither shall any man pluck them out of my hand"—Whitefield exhorted, "O that the words may come to your hearts with as much warmth and power as they did to mine thirty-five years ago."[49] To Whitefield, the perseverance of the saints is the grand crescendo in the symphony of God's plan of salvation: "Some talk of being justified at the day of judgment; that is nonsense; if we are not justified here, we shall not be justified there."[50] He believed justification by faith alone is a finished transaction, settled forever at the moment of conversion.

To those who said that justification is finalized on the last day, Whitefield replied that they built on shifting sand:

"Because the creature thereby is taught, that his being kept in a state of salvation is owing to his own free-will. And what a sandy foundation is that for a poor creature to build his hopes of perseverance upon!"[51] Eternal security is the bedrock truth upon which all true believers build. "He holds them in His hand, that is, He holds them by His power; none shall pluck them thence,"[52] he said. This was the strong gospel message Whitefield offered the multitudes, a gospel that justifies immediately and forever.

Whitefield was bewildered that any believer could doubt or deny the final perseverance of the saints: "I am astonished any poor souls, and good people I hope too, can fight against the doctrine of the perseverance of the saints."[53] Such a doctrinal fallacy stands in direct contradiction to the larger body of biblical truth. With a sense of finality, Whitefield said, "The gifts and callings of God are without repentance. Whom He loves, I am persuaded, He loves to the end."[54] This deep conviction and sure confidence in Whitefield empowered his preaching.

On December 24, 1740, while in Bethesda, Georgia, Whitefield answered his friend John Wesley regarding their controversy surrounding the doctrines of grace. In addition to promoting a synergistic regeneration, where God and man must cooperate in the new birth, Wesley explicitly denied the perseverance of the saints. In his famous letter, Whitefield countered, "This doctrine is my daily support: I should utterly sink under a dread of my impending trials, was I not firmly persuaded that God has chosen me in Christ from before the foundation of the world, and that now being effectually called, He will suffer none to pluck me out of His almighty hand."[55] This is the great significance Whitefield placed upon the eternal security of all believers, a doctrine of foundational importance.

■ ■ ■

The evangelistic zeal of George Whitefield was securely anchored to the doctrines of grace. Whitefield understood that he stood in a long line of godly men who down through the centuries held to divine sovereignty in human salvation. In his biographical account of Whitefield, Stephen Mansfield wrote of such convictions, "Whitefield felt himself standing with Paul and Augustine, Calvin and Luther."[56] Regarding these biblical doctrines, Whitefield knew he stood shoulder-to-shoulder with such other notable figures as John Knox, John Owen, Matthew Henry, John Bunyan, and his contemporaries Jonathan Edwards and John Newton. This great evangelist spoke with one voice alongside these luminaries and countless others down through the centuries.

These grand truths came with great sanctifying power within Whitefield's own soul. Mansfield noted:

For Whitefield, predestination was the greatest reason for humility, obedience, and gratitude. . . . How glorious that preaching is the privilege of harvesting what a man has not planted and cannot grow! This was the glory of Calvinism and Whitefield reveled in it: the freedom from works, the assurance of grace, and the boldness of a man held by God.[57]

It could be said of what Whitefield believed and preached, "It was Calvinism aflame and Whitefield carried it passionately to the nations."[58] This he did perhaps better than any who ever lived.

With ardent desire to see Christ exalted, Whitefield wrote a letter to a friend that best summarized his deep convictions:

The doctrines of our election and free justification in Christ Jesus . . . fill my soul with a holy fire and afford me great confidence in God my Saviour. I hope we shall catch fire from each other and that there shall be a holy emulation amongst us who shall most debase man and exalt the Lord Jesus. Nothing but the Reformation can do this. . . . I know that Christ is all in all. Man is nothing: he hath a free will to go to hell, but none to go to heaven, till God worketh in him to will and do of His good pleasure.[59]

May God restore these transcendent truths in His church again. May He usher in another Great Awakening in these days. As Whitefield stated, nothing but the biblical doctrines of the Reformation can do this.

CHAPTER FOUR

A Gospel without Compromise

Other ministers could, perhaps, preach the Gospel as clearly, and in general say the same things. But, I believe, no man living could say them in his way. Here I always thought him unequalled, and I hardly expect to see his equal while I live.[1]

—JOHN NEWTON

The eighteenth century was an era of great preachers, men whom God raised up to proclaim His Word and mark their generation. A survey of modern-day Christianity would surely identify the greatest preacher in Britain during the period of the evangelical revival as John Wesley, one of the founders of Methodism. Likewise, a polling today of observers of the early American revivals would undoubtedly name Jonathan Edwards, regarded by many as America's greatest pastor-theologian, as the premier preacher of the Great Awakening in the colonies.

However, if you were able to go back in time and survey those living during the eighteenth century, whether in London, in Edinburgh, or in America, there is little doubt that their answer would be one and the same. In fact, even John Wesley or Jonathan Edwards would likely name the same man. The man most widely regarded by his contemporaries as the greatest preacher of his time was George Whitefield.

As a harvester of souls, Whitefield lived to magnify Jesus Christ and call lost sinners to repentance and faith in Him. The focus of his extraordinary ministry was the simple proclamation of the gospel and the appeal to the unconverted to enter through the narrow gate. Wherever he was—whether in a church, in an open field, in a city square, on a ship, in a house—and with whomever he was—whether with royalty, coal miners, the cultured, or the uncouth—Whitefield was unashamedly lifting up Christ and fervently calling for their verdict. He purposed not to be with anyone for more than fifteen minutes without confronting them with the claims of Christ.

At the heart of Whitefield's prolific ministry was this gospel message. He reveled in the truths of the free grace of God in the substitutionary atonement of Christ. Whitefield's own heart had been captured by the gospel while a student at Oxford, and he resolved to take this same life-altering message to the masses. He chose not to wait for the unconverted to come to him. As a shepherd goes after the one lost sheep that has wandered from the fold, Whitefield ardently pursued those lost and in need of Christ. This was the heart of his preaching and the soul of his ministry.

In this chapter, we will focus upon the main elements that defined the evangelistic endeavors of this remarkable revivalist. We will concentrate on the fact that in his gospel ministry, he continually exposed sin, exalted the cross, required regeneration, summoned the will, and pointed to eternity. Here lay the driving forces behind Whitefield's soul-winning efforts. To grasp these essential truths is to understand the dynamics of his ocean-spanning ministry.

EXPOSING SIN

Whitefield was convinced that any presentation of the gospel must begin by exposing the listener's sin and his dire need for salvation. This necessitated the preacher's confronting his hearers' rebellion against God and warning of the eternal consequences of their rejection. Whitefield plainly understood that none rightly desire the gospel of Christ until they know of their own condemnation before God. Whitefield preached those truths that reveal sin, namely, the holiness of God, the fall of Adam, the demands of the law, the curse of disobedience, the certainty of death, the reality of the final judgment, and the eternality of punishment in hell.

When addressing the unregenerate masses, Whitefield sought to ensure that their depravity was fully laid bare.

Martyn Lloyd-Jones aptly stated, "No man could expose the condition of the natural unregenerate heart more powerfully than George Whitefield."[2] Only when confronted with their sinfulness, Whitefield insisted, would unbelievers seek to embrace Christ as their Savior and Lord. He peeled back the outer layers of people's self-righteousness in order to bring about self-awareness of their sinful hearts.

The work of evangelism mandated that he address the eternally devastating effects of sin in his preaching. Whitefield, like a watchman on the tower, warned of sin, death, and judgment. He sought to disturb his listeners with their lost condition before a righteous Judge in heaven. "The sin of your nature, your original sin, is sufficient to sink you into torments, of which there will be no end," he preached. "Therefore unless you receive the Spirit of Christ, you are reprobates, and you cannot be saved."[3] He believed the lost must be driven to the brink of utter desperation before they will come to faith in Christ.

Whitefield was a master at sweeping away all useless rhetoric in order that the unconverted would recognize their desperate need to repent. He implored them, "You are lost, undone, without Him; and if He is not glorified in your salvation, He will be glorified in your destruction; if He does not come and make His abode in your hearts, you must take up an eternal abode with the devil and his angels."[4] None who heard Whitefield were put to sleep with a false sense of security.

Pointing back to Adam's transgression, Whitefield emphasized that all are born with an inherited sin nature from the first man. He declared, "We all stand in need of being justified, on account of the sin of our natures: for we are all chargeable with original sin, or the sin of our first parents."[5] It was this strong belief in original sin and total depravity that caused his every sermon to drive his listeners to grasp a sense of their desperate condition in sin. All humanity is born spiritually dead, he believed:

> Can you deny that you are fallen creatures? Do not you find that you are full of disorders, and that these disorders make you unhappy? Do not you find that you cannot change your own hearts? Have you not resolved many and many a time, and have not your corruptions yet dominion over you? Are you not bondslaves to your lusts, and led captive by the devil at his will?[6]

Whitefield's sermons were filled with vivid warnings of the horrific dangers of remaining in a state of sin. In his sermon "Walking with God," he warned that hell may be but one step away for them: "For how knowest thou, O man, but the next step thou takest may be into hell? Death may seize thee, judgment find thee, and then the great gulf will be fixed between thee and endless glory for ever and ever. O think of these things, all yet that are unwilling to walk with God. Lay them to heart."[7] Whitefield understood that gospel preaching must include the threat of hell, which is intended to drive men to flee to Christ and escape His terrors.

By such strong statements, Whitefield shined a sin-exposing spotlight into the dark crevasses of depraved hearts. Only then would sinners flee to the foot of the cross of the Lord Jesus Christ to hear about a Savior who died for their guilty souls.

EXALTING THE CROSS

Whitefield next proceeded to the saving death of the Lord Jesus Christ. The message of sin is dark, but by it the truth of salvation through the cross shines that much brighter. Few men have ever proclaimed the death of Christ with greater precision and power. Whenever Whitefield preached, he spoke of the perfect atonement accomplished by the death of the Son of God. Moving from man's ruin in sin to Christ's redemption at the cross, Whitefield preached of Christ crucified as his greatest passion and most-dominant note.

Whitefield set before sinners Christ's death and His atoning blood as the only means of salvation. He relentlessly issued the invitation to come to the Savior by faith and find a sufficient substitute for the sins of all who believe in Him:

Our mountains of sins must all fall before this great Zerubbabel. On Him God the Father has laid the iniquities of all that shall believe on Him; and in His own body He bare them on the tree. There, there, by faith, O mourners in Zion, may you see your Savior hanging with arms stretched out, and hear Him, as it were, thus speaking to your souls: "Behold how I have loved you! Behold My hands and My feet! Look, look into My wounded side, and see a heart flaming with love: love stronger than death. Come into My arms, O sinners, come wash your spotted souls in My heart's blood. See here is a fountain opened for all sin and all uncleanness! See, O guilty souls, how the wrath of God is now abiding upon you: come, haste away, and hide yourselves in the clefts of My wounds; for I am wounded for your transgressions; I am dying that you may live forevermore. Behold, as Moses lifted up the serpent in the wilderness, so am I here lifted up upon a tree. See how I am become a curse for you: the chastisement of your peace is upon Me. I am thus scourged, thus wounded, thus crucified, that you by My stripes may be healed. Oh, look unto Me, all you trembling sinners, even to the ends of the earth! Look unto Me by faith, and you shall be saved."[8]

Using vivid language, Whitefield described the sin-bearing terrors of the cross of Christ. He led his listeners back to the scene of the crucifixion of the Lord Jesus. He urged them to look upon the wounded Savior:

Look then, look then, by the eye of faith, to that God-man whom you have pierced. Behold Him bleeding, panting, dying upon the cross, with arms stretched out ready to embrace you all. Hark! How He groans! See how all nature is in agony! The rocks rend, the graves open; the sun withdraws its light, ashamed as it were to see the God of nature suffer; and all this to usher in man's great redemption.[9]

Hear Whitefield again pleaded with his hearers to look to Christ dying upon the cross for sinners, and believe:

Look on His hands, bored with pins of iron; look on His side, pierced with a cruel spear, to let loose the sluices of His blood, and open a fountain for sin, and for all uncleanness . . . only believe in Him, and then, though you have crucified Him afresh, yet will He abundantly pardon you; "though your sins be as scarlet, yet shall they be as wool; though deeper than crimson, yet shall they be whiter than snow."[10]

Whitefield preached best, he perceived, when he proclaimed the glories of the cross. He affirmed, "I am never better than when I am brought to lie at the foot of the cross."[11] Throughout his sermons, journal entries, and correspondence, Whitefield repeatedly exalted the cross as the singular and supreme hope for sinners. Joseph Belcher described Whitefield as a man whose "whole soul was . . . in habitual contact with the cross."[12] It was his constant gazing upon the death of the crucified Savior that drove Whitefield to pursue the lost with the message of grace. Whitefield preached the cross as the saving purpose for which Christ came to this earth.

REQUIRING REGENERATION

Whitefield, moreover, was continually expounding upon the necessity of regeneration, as a "great theme"[13] in his preaching, according to Lloyd-Jones. There is an often-repeated story in which a woman asked Whitefield after a preaching service, "Why do you keep saying to us, 'You must be born again'?" The great evangelist answered, "Because, dear woman, you *must* be born again."[14] This was a central thrust in his many sermons, namely, the absolute necessity of regeneration in order to gain entrance into the kingdom of God.

At the heart of Whitefield's preaching was this doctrine of the new birth. Arnold Dallimore asserted, "Throughout these sermons there runs one great Scriptural truth—the truth indicated by Whitefield when he summarized his early ministry and its effect, saying, 'The doctrine of the New Birth . . . made its way like lightning into the hearers' consciences.' He stood, not as declaring his own message, but that of God as set forth in His Word, 'Ye must be born again.'"[15] Further establishing that the new birth was primary in Whitefield's preaching, Dallimore stated, "The one great truth which had been the foundation of Whitefield's ministry from the first was that of the new birth."[16] Here lay the core of Whitefield's preaching.

Dallimore noted that Whitefield's sermon titled "The Nature and Necessity of the New Birth" was his "most widely circulated discourse."[17] He further stated, "There can be no doubt that the man on the street in Bristol, Gloucester, and London, had he been asked in 1739, 'What do Whitefield and the Methodists believe?' would have answered, 'They claim everybody must be born again.'"[18] Another observer noted the following concerning Whitefield's preaching: "Regeneration was another great doctrine, which the excellent man much insisted upon; hardly a single sermon, but he mentioned it, sometimes more than twice."[19] Henry Stout, professor at Yale University, observed along the same lines that in Whitefield's preaching the new birth is said to be the "chief product."[20]

Regeneration had not been a central focus for the Reformers, but Whitefield made it a dominant emphasis in his preaching. Never allowing it to be relegated to secondary status, the evangelist wrote, "The doctrine of our regeneration or new birth in Christ Jesus . . . [is] one of the most fundamental doctrines of our holy religion" and is "the very hinge on which the salvation of each of us turns."[21] This was a truth repeatedly lifted up and driven home to the hearts of his listeners.

This primary focus upon regeneration goes back to Whitefield's own experience of salvation. While a student at Oxford, he came to know Christ by reading Henry Scougal's *The Life of God in the Soul of Man*. This work explained that salvation is by divine grace, not by man's own self-righteous efforts. As Scougal's title suggests, the reality of regeneration is the life of

God in the soul of man. Once Whitefield was born again, he never forgot this personal experience. He was constantly proclaiming this fundamental truth to his unbelieving listeners.

Whitefield repeatedly asserted the need for his hearers to find identity in Christ alone. Reliance upon denominational ties and religious affiliations, he contended, would simply not suffice. While preaching in Philadelphia, Whitefield exclaimed:

> Father Abraham, who have you in heaven? Any Episcopalians? No. Any Presbyterians? No. Any Baptists? No. Have you any Methodists, Seceders, or Independents there? No, no. Why, who have you there? We don't know those names here. All who are here are Christians, believers in Christ—men who have overcome by the blood of the Lamb, and the Word of His testimony.[22]

Men must be born again, Whitefield asserted, to be made right with God. They must be in Christ "by an inward change and purity of heart and cohabitation of His Holy Spirit."[23] This is by the sovereign operation of God. In regeneration, "God is a sovereign agent. His sacred Spirit blows when and where it wishes."[24] Standing behind the truth on regeneration is the doctrine of election. Whitefield exulted, "[God] will have mercy on whom He will have mercy."[25] Just as there is nothing that man can do to cause his physical birth, there nothing he can do to induce spiritual labor in the new birth.

This is a truth that Whitefield deeply believed and preached as he urged his listeners: you *must* be born again.

SUMMONING THE WILL

Whitefield pressed the hearts of his listeners for an immediate response. It was not enough for him that people knew the truth of the gospel. They must fully commit themselves to Jesus Christ. "Though I hold particular election, yet I offer Jesus freely to every individual soul,"[26] he said. Whitefield was constantly calling men and women to come to Christ.

Martyn Lloyd-Jones implored, "Let us, I hope, once and forever put an end to that lie which says that Calvinism and an interest in evangelism are not compatible."[27] Lloyd-Jones argued that the great evangelists of church history were Calvinistic in their theology: "Here is the greatest evangelist England has ever produced and he was a Calvinist. Charles Haddon Spurgeon, the greatest evangelist of last century, confesses that he had modeled himself—as far as he had modeled himself on anybody—on George Whitefield. And he too was a Calvinist."[28]

Whitefield biographer Lee Gatiss commented, "Every time, [Whitefield] makes an appeal to his listeners to respond to what they have heard in the living and active word of God. His appeals were variously based on the text and could be either invitations to enjoy the benefits spoken of, warnings to escape the wrath to come, pleadings to accept an offer given, or commands to repent and obey a new Lord."[29] As White-field preached, he was summoning his listeners to respond by faith.

It could be argued that Whitefield's favorite word in preaching was the word *come*. He repeatedly urged his listeners to *come* to Christ by faith. Consider the following passionate invitation:

Come, all of you, *come*, and behold Him stretched out for you; see His hands and feet nailed to the cross. O, *come*, *come*, my brethren, and nail your sins thereto. *Come*, *come* and see His side pierced; there is a fountain open for sin, and for uncleanness: O, wash, wash and be clean: *come* and see His head crowned with thorns, and all for you. Can you think of a panting, bleeding, dying Jesus, and not be filled with pity toward Him? He underwent all this for you. *Come* unto Him by faith; lay hold on Him: there is mercy for every soul of you that will *come* unto Him. Then do not delay; fly unto the arms of this Jesus, and you shall be made clean in His blood.[30]

Hear the impassioned pleading of Whitefield as he calls his listeners to respond by faith and come to Christ immediately:

Come, then, unto Christ, everyone that hears me this night; I offer Jesus Christ, pardon, and salvation to all you who will accept thereof. *Come*, O you drunkards; lay aside your cups, drink no more to excel; *come* and drink of the water which Christ will give you, and then you will thirst no more. *Come*, O you thieves; let him that has stolen, steal no more, but fly unto Christ, and He will receive you. *Come* unto Him, O you harlots; lay aside your lusts and turn unto the Lord, and He will have mercy upon you; He will cleanse you of all your sins and wash you in His blood. *Come*, all you liars; *come*, all you Pharisees; *come*, all you fornicators, adulterers, swearers, and blasphemers; *come* to Christ, and He will take away all your filth; He will cleanse you from your pollution, and your sins shall be done away. *Come*, *come*, my guilty brethren; I beseech you for Christ's sake, and for your immortal soul's sake, to *come* unto Christ.[31]

With intense passion and compelling persuasion, Whitefield implored his listeners:

Come, I beseech you to *come* unto Jesus Christ. Oh, that my words would pierce to the very soul! Oh, that Jesus Christ was formed in you! Oh, that you would turn to the Lord Jesus Christ, that he might have mercy upon you! I would speak till midnight, yes, I would speak till I could speak no more, so it might be a means to bring you to Jesus; let the Lord Jesus but enter your souls, and you shall find peace which the world can neither give nor take away.[32]

"Come!" Whitefield exclaimed. Come as guilty, helpless, hell-deserving sinners and find righteousness and life in Christ: "In Him is your only help; fly to Him then by faith; say unto Him, as the poor leper did, 'Lord, if Thou wilt,' Thou canst make me willing; and He will stretch forth the right hand of His power to assist and relive you."[33]

It is quite clear that Whitefield believed an invitation must be offered to the lost to come to Christ. Still, he did not practice an "altar call," nor did he encourage emotional excitement among his congregation. He said, "I offer you salvation this day; the door of mercy is not yet shut, there does yet remain a sacrifice for sin, for all that will accept of the Lord Jesus Christ."[34] This gospel appeal represents countless invitations Whitefield extended to his listeners.

Those under the sound of his voice must not delay even one more moment. Whitefield urged them to act decisively and embrace Jesus Christ who died for sinners:

Make haste then, O sinners, make haste, and *come* by faith to Christ. Then this day, even this hour, nay, this moment, if you believe, Jesus Christ shall come and make His eternal abode in your hearts. . . . Alas! Why do you stand still? How know you, whether Jesus Christ may ever call you again? *Come* then, poor, guilty sinners; *come* away, poor, lost, undone publicans: make haste, I say, and *come* away to Jesus Christ.[35]

Whitefield intensely sought to wake sinners from their spiritual slumber, exhorting them to run to Christ. He did so by arguing that they would have no excuse when they stood before the Judge of all ages:

This day I have invited all, even the worst of sinners, to be married to the Lord Jesus. If you perish, remember you do not perish for lack of invitation. You yourselves shall stand forth at the last day, and I here give you a summons to meet me at the judgment seat of Christ, and to clear both my Master and me. Would weeping, would tears, prevail on you, I could wish my head were waters, and my eyes fountains of tears, that I might weep out every argument and melt you into love. Would anything I could do, or suffer, influence your hearts, I think I could bear to pluck out my eyes, or even to lay down my life, for your sakes.[36]

This was the urgency with which he summoned the human will and urged for a decisive commitment. J. I. Packer remarked that Whitefield's preaching was urging "on-the-spot entries into the reality of the new birth."[37] Here was

Whitefield pleading with his hearers to respond to the gospel and embrace Christ.

POINTING TO ETERNITY

Whitefield further impressed upon his listeners the certain reality of eternity that lay before them. He addressed them with a mighty sense of God and a weighty sense of eternity. He preached as though the final judgment, heaven, and hell were looming on the immediate horizon. In nearly every sermon, Whitefield affirmed that the day of eternity was close at hand. The Judge is standing at the door, he exclaimed, ready to step onto the scene. This kind of eternity-pressing preaching—of both heaven and hell—characterized the evangelistic thrust of George Whitefield.

Whitefield spoke of heaven as a glorious reality and the future home to which all saints will go. He proclaimed, "In heaven the wicked one shall cease from troubling you, and your weary souls shall enjoy an everlasting rest; his fiery darts cannot reach those blissful regions: Satan will never come anymore to appear with, disturb, or accuse the sons of God, when once the Lord Jesus Christ shuts the door."[38] To be free from sin and in the presence of Christ is the supreme blessing of heaven; the great separation will occur, removing believers from unbelievers and righteousness from unrighteousness.

With graphic words and an arresting voice, Whitefield had the keen ability to dramatically represent the horrors of hell. His vivid language in describing the lake of fire caused people to feel as if they might drop into the bottomless pit at any moment. Crying, screaming, and weeping could be heard as Whitefield preached on the fiery punishment of the ungodly. In one sermon, Whitefield challenged his listeners:

> Think often on the pains of hell; consider, whether it is not better to cut off a right hand or foot, and pull out a right eye, if they offend us (or cause us to sin) "rather than to be cast into hell, where the worm dieth not, and the fire is not quenched." Think how many thousands there are now reserved with damned spirits in chains of darkness unto the judgment of the great day. . . . Think you, they now imagine Jesus Christ to be an hard master; or rather think you not, they would give then thousand times ten thousand worlds, could they but return to life again, and take Christ's easy yoke upon them? And can we dwell with everlasting burnings more than they? . . . How shall we bear the irrevocable sentence, "Depart from me, ye cursed, into everlasting fire, prepared for the devil and his angels"?[39]

Whitefield often asked searching questions of his listeners, forcing them to think about where they would spend eternity. By their own answers his hearers would often condemn themselves.

How will you be able to stand at the bar of an angry, sin-avenging Judge and see so many discourses you have despised, so many ministers, who once longed and labored for the salvation of your precious and immortal souls, brought out as so many swift witnesses against you? Will it be sufficient then, think you, to allege that you went to hear them only out of curiosity, to pass away an idle hour, to admire the oratory or ridicule the simplicity of the preacher?[40]

No decision for Christ, Whitefield asserted, could be made after one dies. He pleaded, "While your sins are not repented of, you are in danger of death, and if you should die, you would perish forever. There is no hope of any who live and die in their sins, but that they will dwell with devils and damned spirits to all eternity."[41] Unless lost souls receive Christ in this life, there is no hope in the eternal ages that one should escape the punishment of the damned.

So powerful were Whitefield's pleas in his sermons that "scoffers were put to silence, and Satan's strongholds were pulled down."[42] On one occasion at a drinking club in Philadelphia, it is recounted that there was a boy "who used to mimic people for their diversion. Persuaded by the gentlemen, the boy (though reluctantly) stood up and mimicked Whitefield, and said, 'I speak the truth in Christ, I lie not; unless you repent you will all be damned.' This unexpected speech (quoted from one of Whitefield's sermons) broke up the club, which has never met since."[43] Though physically absent, Whitefield's pressing appeals nevertheless resounded through the bars and back alleys of every town in which he preached.

Whitefield's alarming message to his audience was that if they did not believe in Christ, their lost souls would surely enter an eternity of God's wrath: "Oh sinner! I beseech you to repent, let not the wrath of God be awakened! Let not the fires of eternity be kindled against you!"[44] His fervor led him to press hard upon the hearts of his hearers the realities of both heaven and hell. Whitefield always lived in light of eternity and preached as one who sensed the impending day drawing ever nearer.

■ ■ ■

The evangelistic zeal of George Whitefield flowed out of his love for the glorious gospel of grace. It was this supreme love and devotion that drove him to pursue the lost, expose sin, exalt the cross, summon the will, and point to eternity. Thoroughly Calvinistic in theology, this fervent evangelist held forth the only saving message there is for guilty sinners. He delighted in calling them to faith in Christ and leaving the results to God, who alone can save.

Arnold Dallimore wrote, "His ministry presents an unparalleled example of declaring the sovereignty of God combined with the free offer of salvation to all who would believe on Christ."[45] Whitefield provides the quintessential example of one who held the doctrines of grace in one hand and the free offer of the gospel in the other hand. To know this about Whitefield is to know the man, and to know the man is to have a most excellent example to follow.

We need to have a similar granite-like boldness in our gospel message. We need to go back to Paul, to Augustine, to Luther, Calvin, and the Reformers, to the Puritans, and ultimately back to Whitefield. We need again heralds such as these, those who are not ashamed to preach sin and judgment, heaven and hell, repentance and faith, righteousness and holiness. We must preach the necessity of radical life transformation that can only come about through the reality of the new birth.

May God raise up in this day a host of such clarion voices that will proclaim this same gospel message.

CHAPTER FIVE

A Passion
That Consumed

*The plain truth is, that the Church of England of that
day was not ready for a man like Whitefield. The Church
was too much asleep to understand him, and was vexed at
a man who would not keep still and let the devil alone.*[1]

—J. C. RYLE

On the morning of October 23, 1740, in a field of Kensington Parish, near what is today Berlin, Connecticut, a colonial farmer named Nathan Cole received the news that the great evangelist George Whitefield would be preaching in the nearby city of Middletown. Immediately, he dropped his tools and ran to his house, hastily grabbing his wife and saddling his horse, and rushed to the announced site of Whitefield's meeting twelve miles away. Cole and his wife alternated between riding and running to Middletown, for he simply *must* be present to hear this celebrated preacher.

Still quite a distance from the city, Cole and his wife observed the hillsides covered in what seemed to be a swelling, mist-like fog.[2] As they traveled closer, they discovered the low cloud was dust from the road as a flood of people descended upon Middletown by horse and carriage. Eager to hear Whitefield preach, some four thousand people had already assembled at the town square. Cole stood amid the crowd and watched the evangelist make his appearance. He later admitted, "When I saw Mr. Whitefield come upon the scaffold, he looked almost angelic."[3] He described Whitefield as "a young, slim, slender youth before thousands of people, and with bold undaunted countenance."[4] The talk circulating among the great crowd was, "God was with him everywhere."

As Whitefield began to preach, Cole sensed a great fear gripping his soul. The preaching came with much power upon this farmer's unconverted heart. Cole said the young preacher "looked as if he was clothed with authority from the Great God, and a sweet solemnity sat upon his brow." He further testified, "My hearing him preach gave me a heart wound. By God's blessing, my old foundation was broken up, and I saw that my righteousness would not save me."[5] The full force of Whitefield's preaching proved to be irresistible. Cole would look back to this day in Middletown as the time when God laid the hammer to his hardened heart and began to convict him of his sin and draw him to Himself.

Such was the case for many who heard Whitefield preach. They not only heard him, but *felt* the pathos of the man. Even

Jonathan Edwards, a towering intellectual figure, wept on the front pew as Whitefield preached in Northampton. Such an account reveals much about the force of Whitefield's preaching. In a day when pulpit delivery had degenerated into dry ritual, involving nothing more than a monotone reading of a sermon manuscript, Whitefield burst onto the scene with intense *preaching*. That is to say, this celebrated evangelist came exhorting, pleading, wooing, calling, begging, even weeping before his listeners. With deep emotions, his heart bled as he declared the gospel. He spoke with demonstrative body language and commanding gestures that loomed larger than life. Whitefield was aglow with the glory of God as he proclaimed the gospel of Christ.

What marked the intense fervency of Whitefield's preaching? What were the elements of the warm emotion with which he spoke? In this chapter, we want to consider the distinguishing features of the consuming fire that brightly burned within his heart and spread to others, namely, his deep convictions, blood earnestness, fiery zeal, fervent love, and crusading intensity.

DEEP CONVICTIONS

Whitefield's passion arose from the depth of his biblical convictions. Strong beliefs were first ignited in his heart at the moment of his conversion. These firmly held truths were cultivated over the years through intense prayer and diligent study of the Word. Many preachers have weak convictions and therefore have little passion. However, George Whitefield possessed a deep persuasion about the truth, which in turn fueled his passion in preaching. His beliefs in the gospel of sovereign grace stoked the flames of his heart into a blazing furnace.

J. C. Ryle rightly stated, "[Whitefield] succeeded in showing people that he believed all he was saying, and that his heart, and soul, and mind, and strength, were bent on making them believe it too."[6] Even under the flurry of rotten tomatoes thrown while he preached, dead cats being tossed onto the platform, and the obnoxious noises of disruption, Whitefield was nevertheless propelled forward throughout his ministry by his rock-solid conviction in the truth. Whether in an open field, a house, or a ship, Whitefield believed that he preached by divine appointment. The reputation of his boldness and conviction went before him, and revival followed in his wake.

Whenever he stood behind an open Bible, Whitefield was thoroughly convinced that he was delivering divine truth. He firmly believed he was feeding the bread of life to starving beggars. This inner conviction created flaming passion in his preaching. Like a tree rooted in rich soil, Whitefield could not be moved. He remained firm in the cardinal doctrines he believed are essential for salvation. When he spoke, he used plain words to address every rank and condition among his listeners. He did so with the certainty that he was a divinely appointed spokesman for God, bringing His truth on His behalf:

I thank God, I am so far from changing my principles, which I am sure I was taught by God's word and Spirit, that I am more and more confirmed, that if I was to die this moment, I hope I should have strength and courage given me to say, I am more convinced of the efficacy and the power of those truths which I preached when I was twenty years old, than when I first preached them.[7]

These convictions caused Whitefield to speak with the authority of God Himself. He believed he had been sent by God to bring the divine message recorded in the infallible Scriptures. This belief deepened his passion when he spoke. He preached not his own opinions, but the very wisdom of God, which shook his hearers from their doldrums:

"If I had come to speak to you in my own name, you might rest your elbows upon your knees, and your heads upon your hands, and sleep; and once in a while look up and say, 'What does this babbler talk of?' But I have not come to you in my own name. No, I have come to you in the name of the Lord God of Hosts, and"—here he brought down his hand and foot at once, so as to make the whole house ring—"and I must and will be heard." Everyone in the house started, the old father, who always slept, among the rest. "Aye, aye," continued the preacher, looking at him, "I have waked you up, have I? I meant to do it. I am not come here to preach to stocks and stones; I am come to you in the name of the Lord God of Hosts, and I must and will have an audience."[8]

Such immovable convictions in Whitefield held sway over his listeners' hearts. Even unbelievers were drawn to the force of his firm belief in the truth. David Hume, the Scottish philosopher and skeptic, was even challenged as he was seen going to hear George Whitefield preach: "I thought you do not believe in the gospel," someone said to him. Hume replied, "I don't, but he does."[9] It was this overwhelming conviction in the truth of God's Word that attracted large multitudes like a magnet to listen to him preach.

BLOOD EARNESTNESS

Whitefield preached with a deep sobriety, or what could be called blood earnestness. Each time he mounted the pulpit, he was gripped in his soul that the eternal destinies of men were hanging in the balance. He knew the message he brought was the most important truth his listeners would ever hear. He preached the weighty message of a crucified Savior who secured eternal salvation for hell-bound sinners. Such preaching must be marked by gravity, not levity, and solemnity, not apathy.

The seriousness with which Whitefield approached preaching was apparent to all. He proclaimed the gospel, Gillies noted, with "a solemnity of manner" that conveyed "a sense of the importance of what he was about to say."[10] J. C. Ryle concurred, noting the "tremendous earnestness"[11] in Whitefield's preaching. Ian Paisley added, "Whitefield was in deadly earnest. He preached as one who 'had measured eternity and taken the dimensions of a soul.'"[12] Such *gravitas* was the burden of the Lord upon his soul and brought soberness to his pulpit delivery.

With intense passion, Whitefield believed his time to preach God's Word was short. On one occasion, he noted, "I found about a thousand souls waiting till eight in the evening to hear the Word. Though nature said, 'Spare thyself,' I thought faith and duty said, 'Venture upon the Lord's strength, and speak to them.' I did, from these words of our dear Lord's: 'I must work the works of Him that sent me, while it is day: the night cometh when no man can work.'"[13] Whitefield preached every sermon as if it were his last message. He poured himself into every truth that proceeded from his mouth.

Though he often preached under the threat of his own life, danger only increased Whitefield's earnestness. Recounting one particular occasion, Whitefield remarked:

I narrowly escaped with my life; for as I was passing from the pulpit to the coach, I felt my wig and hat to be almost off. I turned about, and observed a sword just touching my temples. A young rake, as I afterwards found, was determined to stab me, but a gentleman, seeing the sword thrusting near me, struck it up with his cane, and so the destined victim providentially escaped.[14]

From the beginning of his ministry, Whitefield determined in his heart that he would preach the gospel no matter the peril. Not only were the lives of his listeners in God's hands, but so was his own.

The grim reality of death caused him to preach as though his listeners stood on the brink of eternity, ready to step into either heaven or hell. So earnest was Whitefield, Ian Paisley explained, that "the congregation saw only a prophet beholding the very throne of God, and on terms of familiarity with celestial beings. He preached with such earnestness in describing the soul as a ship-wrecked vessel with masts gone, on her beam ends, that when he asked, 'What?' The sailors in his congregation frantically responded 'Take to the long boat!'"[15] At the close of one sermon in Edinburgh, Whitefield thrust upon his congregation the reality of their own imminent deaths and immediate appearance before God:

> "The attendant angel is just about to leave this threshold and ascend to heaven; and shall he ascend and not bear with him the news of one sinner, among all this multitude reclaimed from the error of his ways?"

Then with uplifted hands and eyes to heaven he cried, "Stop, Gabriel! Stop, Gabriel! Stop ere you enter the sacred portals, and yet carry with you the news of one sinner converted to God!"[16]

Whitefield so elevated the importance of preaching that he stated, "May I die preaching."[17] Again, "I hope yet to die in the pulpit, or soon after I come out of it."[18] In God's providence, Whitefield realized this very desire. On a balcony not far from his deathbed, he preached his last sermon to a large crowd that had filled the street in front of the parsonage. He died within hours of extending the invitation for all to embrace Christ.

Fiery Zeal

Whitefield's soul was ignited with fiery zeal in his preaching. His zealous preaching cannot be explained, as some have attempted, by his youthful days on the theatrical stage or by his higher education at Oxford. To the contrary, Whitefield was full of fire and fervor in his preaching because he was so full of God. John Carrick wrote, "As he preached his whole person became alive in a powerful . . . movement of body, the expression of his countenance, and modulations of his voice."[19] J. I. Packer added that Whitefield possessed an "arms-lifted, foot-stamping passion . . . with an overflow of compassionate affection."[20] Amos Stevens Billingsley succinctly stated, "Whitefield was a flame of fire"[21] who burned brightly for the glory of God.

John Gillies noted that Whitefield's preaching possessed "an extraordinary degree of earnestness and zeal."[22] That is, his passion far exceeded any normal measure of soul intensity. "Whitefield preached like a lion," Gillies asserted. "The force and vehemence and passion of that oratory awed the hearers, and made them tremble like Felix before the apostle."[23] Consequently, Whitefield's listeners did not merely hear him preach—they *felt* him: "Many, I trust, have felt, and will long feel the impressions of his zeal and fire, the passion and flame of his expressions."[24]

No one better describes Whitefield's passionate sermon delivery than his gospel co-laborer John Wesley. This former classmate noted that Whitefield spoke with "divine pathos," meaning God-aroused emotions that provoked feelings in others. Moreover, Wesley said his friend preached with "fervency of zeal, that was unequalled since the days of the apostles."[25] The power of Whitefield's preaching, Wesley maintained, "was not the force of education; no, nor the advice of his friends. It was no other than faith in a bleeding Lord."[26] Whitefield spoke with "eloquence" and an "astonishing force of persuasion, which the most hardened sinners could not resist."[27]

Others who heard Whitefield preach described his delivery as "passionate, intense, fiery, and zealous." "Whitefield tended to speak with his hands as much as with his lips and mouth,"[28] Martyn Lloyd-Jones remarked. In fact, Whitefield often preached with a flood of tears as he cried for sinners to embrace Christ. Such affection could hardly be resisted by his listeners. One observer noted:

> I could hardly bear such unreserved use of tears, and the scope he gave to his feelings; for sometimes he exceedingly wept, stamped loudly and passionately, and was frequently so overcome, that for a few seconds, you would suspect he never could recover; and when he did, nature required some little time to compose herself. I hardly ever knew him go through a sermon without weeping more or less, and I truly believe his were tears of sincerity.[29]

Impassioned, fiery, and dramatic, Whitefield's preaching came with depth of passion that welled up within his soul. When criticized for his display of emotions, he responded, "You blame me for weeping, but how can I help it when you will not weep for yourselves, though your immortal souls are on the verge of destruction, and for aught you know, you are hearing your last sermon, and may never more have an opportunity to have Christ offered to you?"[30] Deep within, Whitefield felt the impact of the truth he preached. He proclaimed grace, faith, hell, heaven, and eternity because he believed them to be divine realities.

In every sermon, Whitefield threw a lifeline to those who were drowning in the ocean of their own sin, imploring them to take hold and be saved from perishing. This demanded a note of urgency on his part. To the very end, Whitefield preached with "a frequency and a fervor, that seemed to exceed the natural strength of the most robust."[31] He never mellowed, but remained marked "by fervent zeal, and by a formidable and most persuasive delivery."[32]

On November 11, 1770, John Newton, author of the timeless hymn "Amazing Grace," preached a sermon commemorating the death of Whitefield. Newton likened Whitefield's preaching to a burning light that brought warmth to those who sat under him. "Whether we consider the warmth of his zeal, the greatness of his ministerial talents, or the extensive usefulness with which the Lord honored him . . . ," Newton said, "he was raised up to shine in a dark place."[33]

Whitefield's zealous preaching stood in stark contrast to the lethargic practice of his day. The pulpits of the eighteenth century were severely lacking in passion, zeal, and virtually any force of conviction. Preachers had been cooled by the humanistic philosophies of the hour, which lulled their once-zealous proclamations into a lifeless stupor. Stephen Mansfield noted, "The sermon had been entombed as a religious art form. . . . When Whitefield arrived on the scene, he rescued it. He made it what it ought to have been all along: a desperate plea to a perishing people, a confrontation with the word of the living God."[34]

Anglican ministers of the day were calm, controlled, dignified, sophisticated, and stuffy in their preaching. However, Whitefield was starkly different. He burst onto the scene with a new style of heartfelt fervency not witnessed since the grand age of the Puritans. With glowing affections, Whitefield raised and restored the preaching standard for future generations of Protestant pulpits to this present day.

FERVENT LOVE

Whitefield's intense passion was kindled by his own deepening love for God and Jesus Christ, which in turn ignited his compassion for lost sinners. Biographer Joseph Belcher described Whitefield as being "fired with love, from being in habitual contact with the cross."[35] Whitefield's affection for God was stoked by reflection upon the greatness of His character. Moreover, his heart of love was fueled by his personal communion with Jesus Christ. This intimate knowledge of Christ was the consistent theme that filled his soul and increased his affections. Belcher added that Whitefield was consumed with "a heart burning with love and zeal for his Lord and Master."[36]

Fervent love lay at the very center of Whitefield's effectiveness as an evangelist. As he preached, his love for sinners seemed to overpower them. "In all his discourses," John Gillies observes, "there was a fervent and melting charity, and earnestness of persuasion, an outpouring of redundant love."[37]

Whitefield often wept as he preached. Marcus Loane wrote, "Few could withstand the sight. It woke up affections and touched the hidden strings of the heart as nothing else could ever do; men could not hate one who loved and wept for their souls."[38] He was so compelled by the love of Christ that he found it quite difficult to stop pleading for his listeners' souls.

A deep compassion for unbelievers moved Whitefield in his preaching. He once declared, "The love of Jesus Christ constrains me to lift up my voice like a trumpet. My heart is now full; out of the abundance of the love which I have for your precious and immortal souls, my mouth now speaks; and I could now not only continue my discourse until midnight, but I could speak until I could speak no more."[39] He expended himself wholeheartedly in the pursuit of the lost, and they knew it, and were drawn to his sincere pleas.

The ruling principle of Whitefield's heart was the love of Christ demonstrated at the cross. "The love of Jesus . . . is unfathomable," he declared. "O the height, the depth, the length, and breadth, of this love, that brought the King of Glory from His throne, to die for such rebels as we are, when we had acted so unkindly against Him, and deserved nothing but eternal damnation."[40] This contagious affection for sinners flowed out of Whitefield's conviction that Christ loves indiscriminately all those who come to Him in faith.

No matter the severity of sinners' moral pollution, Whitefield proclaimed the love of Christ to pardon even the most vile and filthy of transgressors. Despite their wickedness, he extended passionate appeals to come to Christ for cleansing from sins. "Why fear ye that the Lord Jesus Christ will not accept you?"[41] he asked. Whitefield desired to remove all hesitation in the unconverted that would prevent them from coming to Christ:

> Your sins will be no hindrance, your unworthiness no hindrance; if your own corrupt hearts do not keep you back nothing will hinder Christ from receiving of you. He loves to see poor sinners coming to Him, He is pleased to see them lie at His feet pleading His promises; and if you thus come to Christ, He will not send you away without His Spirit; no, but will receive and bless you.[42]

The unconditional love of Christ for sinners was a strong catalyst in Whitefield's preaching: "My friends, I trust I feel somewhat of a sense of God's distinguishing love upon my heart! Therefore I must . . . invite poor Christless sinners to come to Him, and accept of His righteousness, that they may have life."[43]

Such divine love drove him to preach to those in need of Christ. His ardent preaching became the conduit through which his love for people flowed. Perhaps it was this very element that caused his ministry to flourish on the world stage. He extended himself indiscriminately to the rich and poor, to duchess and pauper alike. There can be no real understanding of Whitefield's evangelistic preaching without grasping this foundational reality of his love of God ruling in his soul.

CRUSADING INTENSITY

An understanding of Whitefield's ministry must recognize his relentless pursuit of the lost. The eighteenth-century world had never witnessed a preacher like this who would not be confined within the walls of a church building, but instead launched out into the world. In describing this bold initiative, J. C. Ryle noted:

> He was the first to see that Christ's ministers must do the work of fishermen. They must not wait for souls to come to them, but must go after souls, and "compel them to come in." He did not sit tamely by his fireside. . . . He dived into holes and corners after sinners. He hunted out ignorance and vice wherever they could be found. In short, he set on foot a system of action which, up to his time, had been comparatively unknown.[44]

Like Jesus and His Apostles, Whitefield set out onto the open seas of humanity to become a fisher of men. "The whole world is now my parish," he exclaimed. "Wheresoever my Master calls me I am ready to go and preach the everlasting Gospel."[45]

Unwavering in his resolve, Whitefield would not be deterred by any difficulty or opposition from preaching everywhere his foot landed. Of Whitefield's travels, John Newton said, "This messenger of good tidings preached the everlasting gospel in almost every considerable place in England, Scotland, Ireland, and throughout the British empire in America, which is an extent of more than one thousand miles."[46] Even during the time of horse and carriage rides, demanding sea voyages, and arduous travel conditions, Whitefield allowed nothing to prevent him from spreading the good news of Christ to all around him.

Whitefield is remembered as one of the first to preach to African slaves in the colonies. Historian Thomas Kidd commented, "Whitefield expressed growing awareness and concern for the plight of African Americans in both the North and South."[47] Whitefield had, Kidd wrote, "lofty hopes" of educating African slaves with spiritual instruction.[48] Erskine Clarke, in his epic work *Our Southern Zion*, noted the perilous climate into which Whitefield stepped: "Whitefield arrived in Charlestown in January 1740, less than four months after the Stono slave rebellion had been crushed. Fugitive rebels were still at large and another slave conspiracy, brewing in Berkeley County, would break out in a few months."[49] In these dangerous and tumultuous times, as "the fires of the Great Awakening swept across the [South Carolina] low country,"[50] Whitefield went to the slaves and preached Christ.

The first published African American woman, Phillis Wheatley, composed a vivid poem about George Whitefield after his death. Lady Huntingdon, whose personal chaplain Whitefield had become, was a family friend of the Wheatleys and later financed the publication of Phillis's volume of poems.

The poem paid tribute to Whitefield as an instrument used by God to bring a message of hope to a people in the midst of distress. In memorial of this man who extended the love of God to the American slaves, seventeen-year-old Wheatley recognized the compassion he showed to the enslaved by presenting to them the message of eternal life:

> Take HIM, "my dear AMERICANS," he said,
> Be your complaints in His kind bosom laid:
> Take HIM ye *Africans*, He longs for you;
> Impartial SAVIOUR, is His title due;
> If you will chose to walk in grace's road,
> You shall be sons, and kings, and priests to GOD.[51]

Without distinction or prejudice, whether free or slave, Whitefield saw *all* men as enslaved to sin, and he pursued them with indiscriminate determination in order to show the way to what Wheatley called "grace's road." He elevated those who were enslaved and recognized them as precious souls whom God calls to be His children. In Whitefield's preaching, "whosoever will" remained an continual note that he struck.

■ ■ ■

In this chapter, we have noted Whitefield's intense passion in preaching. His deep convictions, blood earnestness, fiery zeal, fervent love, and crusading intensity show him to be a man sanctioned by God to proclaim the unsearchable riches of divine truth. Such a mandate should make any man intense. This was its undeniable effect upon Whitefield's soul. He tells the following story that best demonstrates this point:

> The Archbishop of Canterbury in the year 1675 was acquainted with Mr. Butterton the [actor]. One day the Archbishop . . . said to Butterton . . . "pray inform me Mr. Butterton, what is the reason you actors on stage can affect your congregations with speaking of things imaginary, as if they were real, while we in church speak of things real, which our congregations only receive as if they were imaginary?" "Why my Lord," says Butterton, "the reason is very plain. We actors on stage speak of things imaginary, as if they were real and you in the pulpit speak of things real as if they were imaginary.[52]

Whitefield then made the application to his own life, saying: "Therefore, I will bawl [shout loudly], I will not be a velvet-mouthed preacher."[53]

Preaching with his whole heart, Whitefield was fully engaged in all that he said. That is why on one occasion he told his listeners, "I shall return home with a heavy heart, unless some of you will arise and come to my Jesus; I desire to preach Him and not myself; rest not in hearing and following me."[54] With that, he begged and pleaded with his listeners to believe upon Christ and be saved.

It is this kind of passionate preaching that we need again in this present hour. We could certainly do with fewer stale, exegetical lectures in the pulpit. Save these for the classroom. We could do with fewer frivolous, lighthearted personalities in the pulpit. Instead, what is desperately needed in this day are more intensely urgent pleas and pressing appeals as exemplified by this gifted evangelist, George Whitefield.

A Mandate from the Lord

Whitefield tells us more than anything else—orthodoxy is not enough. . . . In a sense John Calvin always needs George Whitefield. What I mean is this. The danger of those who follow the teachings of Calvin, and do so rightly, is that they tend . . . to sink into what I would describe as an "ossified orthodoxy." And that is of no value, my friend. You need the power of the Spirit upon it.[1]

—MARTYN LLOYD-JONES

In 1753, Samuel Davies, Jonathan Edwards' successor as president of Princeton University, and the Presbyterian minister Gilbert Tennent set sail from America. They were headed to England on a mission to raise money for the fledgling institution. Their journey across the Atlantic was a turbulent sea voyage during which they feared being shipwrecked several times. At last they arrived in London on a Saturday morning.

They immediately sought to know, "Is Mr. Whitefield in town?" To their delight, they were told he was due to preach the next morning. With great anticipation, these two spiritual leaders went to hear Whitefield preach.

Reflecting upon the service, Davies wrote, "It became clear to me quite soon in the service that Mr. Whitefield must have had an exceptionally busy week; obviously he had not had time to prepare his sermon properly." He added, "From the standpoint of construction and ordering of thought it was very deficient and defective; it was a poor sermon. . . . But," he said, "the unction that attended it was such that I would gladly risk the rigours of shipwreck in the Atlantic many times over in order to be there just to come under its gracious influence."[2]

Davies became a spectator of the power of the Holy Spirit that so recognizably fueled the preaching ministry of George Whitefield. Here was a man endued with mighty influence from God as he carried out his proclamation of the Word. As Whitefield stood to declare the gospel, he was made strong in the Lord. The empowering of the Spirit enabled this gifted evangelist to accomplish a monumental work and to witness amazing results.

The effect of the Spirit's influence in Whitefield's life cannot be overstated. It was this divine might that enabled him to traverse the landscape of the British Isles and travel throughout the American colonies proclaiming Jesus Christ. And it was by the Spirit's power that he saw two continents come under the sway of the gospel.

Whitefield believed it was crucial that the Holy Spirit be an experiential reality in his life and ministry. On the 250th anniversary of Whitefield's birth, Northern Irish pastor Ian Paisley noted Whitefield's belief that "the power of God, the Holy Ghost, must be manifested and can be experienced."[3] Whitefield himself asserted, "Believers can feel the Spirit of God in His sanctifying and saving impressions and witnessing with our own spirits."[4] Any observer of Whitefield's expansive ministry would rightly conclude that this itinerant evangelist was endowed with an unusual measure of divine power from the Holy Spirit.

In this concluding chapter, our focus will be upon the power of the Holy Spirit in the preaching ministry of George Whitefield. We will consider how, having received a mission from the Lord, Whitefield was sovereignly called, relentlessly driven, spiritually energized, divinely comforted, and supernaturally effective.

SOVEREIGNLY CALLED

Whitefield believed God had sovereignly called him to preach the gospel. He could not explain his ministry apart from this divine work within him. Initially terrified at the thought of preaching, he would not have chosen this role. Lloyd-Jones commented, "He felt it was such a sacred task; and who was he to enter into a pulpit and to preach? He felt he would run a thousand miles away in order not to preach. Such was his view of it all, and such was his view of himself and his own unworthiness, that it took a great deal to persuade George Whitefield to enter a pulpit and preach."[5]

The Spirit overcame his fears and apprehensions. In the depths of his soul, Whitefield knew he had been called by the Spirit to preach—and preach he *must*. Reflecting on his calling to ministry, Whitefield said he knew it was the Spirit who had summoned him to preach:

> I went to Oxford without a friend; I had not a servant, I had not a single person to introduce me; but God, by his Holy Spirit, was pleased to raise me up to preach for his great name's sake: through his divine Spirit I continue to this day and feel my affections are as strong as ever toward the work and the people of the living God.[6]

Once converted, Whitefield immediately possessed a full assurance that God had sovereignly called him to Himself. Likewise, he was persuaded that he had been empowered for gospel ministry. His sermons were Spirit-charged, and it was obvious to his hearers that it was God speaking when he opened his mouth to preach.

Whitefield believed that many ministers in the Church of England were unconverted and uncalled. These unregenerate preachers had not been divinely appointed to ministry and preached empty and lifeless messages. J. I. Packer said,

"Anglican clergy were writing and reading flat sermons of a mildly moralistic and apologetic sort."[7]

In stark contrast to this hollow rhetoric, Whitefield preached in a fashion that more resembled the Apostles. Packer further explained:

> Whitefield preached extempore about heaven and hell, sin and salvation, the dying love of Christ, and the new birth, clothing his simple expository outlines with glowing dramatic conscience-challenging rhetoric, and reinforcing his vocal alternations of soothing and punching with a great deal of body movement and gesture, thereby adding great energy to the things he was saying.[8]

It was the Holy Spirit who quickened Whitefield's mind, ignited his soul, inflamed his heart, fueled his passion, and strengthened his body. His preaching reintroduced the old truths of Scripture back into the dry atmosphere of gospel preaching. He employed all his gifts and talents to this sacred task. But only the Spirit's calling and gifting can explain the extent of Whitefield's impact.

RELENTLESSLY DRIVEN

Propelled by the power of the Holy Spirit, Whitefield stormed forward into ministry. The relentless drive of Whitefield's herculean effort was fueled by power from on high. Consider the unparalleled pace of Whitefield's itinerant ministry. No matter what lay before him, be it an opportunity or an obstacle, Whitefield's spiritual determination could not be quenched. If denied access to a church pulpit, he would take to the open field. If persecuted by an angry mob, he would persevere despite threats to his safety and life. If preaching on one continent, he would board a ship and sail to the other side of the Atlantic. This persistent herald possessed an assiduous drive to proclaim Christ as few ever have.

Whitefield's productivity extended beyond his preaching. He gave myriad personal interviews with individuals who sought his counsel and kept up a prodigious letter-writing ministry. He founded three churches and one school, and founded and assumed responsibility for an orphanage in Savannah, Georgia. He said, "I ought to lay myself out more and more in going about endeavoring to do good to precious and immortal souls."[9] His heart so overflowed for others that he was compelled to bring them God's Word. Such was Whitefield's resolve.

The endless demands upon his life stretched him beyond his limits. This "inter-continental gospel preacher"[10] was an indefatigable evangelist, often preaching five or six times a day, for as much as forty hours a week. Travel in the eighteenth century was arduous, and Whitefield's schedule—going from city to city, country to country, even continent to continent—would have used up any other man. It is remarkable that he lived as long as he did under such an exacting load.

Whitefield was often urged by others to slow the pace of his ministry. A typical response was, "I would sooner wear out, than rust out."[11] He simply could not shorten his stride, even as his time on earth drew to a close. As Whitefield prepared to deliver what would be his final sermon, someone said to him, "Sir, you are more fit to go to bed than to preach." Whitefield looked up to the heavens and said, "Lord Jesus, I am weary in Thy work, but not of Thy work."[12] Though depleted by his stupendous labors in gospel ministry, Whitefield stepped forward to finish the course that had been set before him.

The only way Whitefield could endure all he did, travel as much as he did, preach as much as he did, and exert the energy that he did, was through the empowerment of the Holy Spirit. Whitefield continually testified to that effect in his *Journals*: "God enabled me to speak with the demonstration of the Spirit, and with power."[13] On another occasion he remarked, "Preached . . . with such demonstration of the Spirit as I never spoke before. . . . God has given me a double portion of His Spirit indeed."[14] Amid his exhausting pace, Whitefield once remarked, "Slept but little tonight, as well as the night before; but was much strengthened by the Holy Spirit."[15] In his own weakness, the Spirit gave him supernatural power to make up what was lacking physically, emotionally, and spiritually.

To the very end, Whitefield was relentlessly driven by the Holy Spirit to accomplish all his hands set out to do. His effectiveness lay not merely in his eloquence or zeal, but arose from the fact that God had "granted upon him and his ministry 'a mighty effusion of the Holy Ghost'; and it was this, the Divine power, which was the first secret of his success."[16]

Spiritually Energized

Whitefield demonstrates that neither mere assent to the truth, nor doctrinal correctness, is enough for effective gospel influence. There must be the empowerment of the Spirit to accompany this truth, both in the preacher and the listener. As Whitefield wrote: "Oh, how Divine truths make their own way, when attended by Divine power."[17] Any power Whitefield possessed did not come from his innate human abilities, but from the Spirit who lived within him.

"Orthodoxy is not enough," Martyn Lloyd-Jones wrote. "There were orthodox men in [Whitefield's] time, but they were comparatively useless. You can have a dead orthodoxy."[18] Reflecting on the Spirit's work in Whitefield, Lloyd-Jones added:

The power of the Spirit is essential. We must be orthodox, but God forbid us to rest even on orthodoxy. We must seek the power of the Spirit that was given to George Whitefield. That will give us a sorrow for souls and a concern for souls, and give us the zeal, and enable us to preach with power and conviction to all classes and kinds of men.[19]

Whitefield's deep love for the souls of men and women did not originate in himself. It was God who gave him an uncommon love for those to whom he preached.

The Spirit also gave Whitefield endurance to accomplish more and more. To a minister in Charleston, South Carolina, he wrote, "I have been enabled to prepare nine discourses for the press. My body waxes stronger; and, last night, the great God, in a glorious manner, filled and overshadowed my soul. I am panting for the complete holiness of Jesus my Lord."[20] There is no explanation for what Whitefield accomplished apart from the power of God in his life.

Even when he felt despair by looking at his adverse circumstances and trials, Whitefield gained strength from the Spirit in order to persevere steadfastly. On one occasion, he recounted:

> Through infinite mercy, I am enabled to strengthen myself in the Lord my God. I am cast down, but not destroyed; perplexed, but not in despair. A few days ago in reading Beza's *Life of Calvin*, these words were much pressed upon me, "Calvin is turned out of Geneva, but, behold a new church arises!" Jesus, the ever loving, altogether lovely Jesus, pities and comforts me.[21]

At another time, Whitefield wrote, "I have been enabled to preach twice daily, and to ride several miles. Congregations have been surprisingly large; the word is attended with power, and the alarm in the country rather greater than ever."[22] From Gloucester on February 5, 1742, he wrote, "Yesterday, I preached three times, and visited a private Society in the evening. Today, I was enabled to preach three times, with great power. Here there is such an awakening, as I never saw in these parts before."[23] Though physically exhausted and mentally drained from the previous days' rigors, Whitefield was spiritually energized for each new day: "I seem to have a new body, and the Lord greatly enriches my soul."[24] Time and again, Whitefield attributed his effectiveness, influence, and scope in ministry to the quickening effect of the Holy Spirit.

The Spirit also gave Whitefield resilience in the face of opposition to the message he preached. He wrote of little boys and girls pelting him eggs and dirt,[25] and recounted that on another occasion, "A few poor souls began to insult me, but Jesus strengthened me much. Several clods were thrown, one of them fell on my head, and another struck my fingers, while I was in prayer. A sweet gospel spirit was given to me."[26]

When faced with such opposition, Whitefield felt as though he was opposing Satan himself. No human messenger relying upon his own strength, Whitefield contended, could ever expect to succeed in direct confrontation with the evil one. He understood the Apostle John's words: "Greater is he that is in you than he that is in the world" (1 John 4:4). The power of the Holy Spirit made him an overcomer in his conflict with the prince of the power of the air. Of one such conflict with the Devil, Whitefield remarked:

Went to St. Helen's, where Satan withstood me greatly—for on a sudden I was deserted, and my strength went from me. But I thought it was the Devil's doing, and therefore was resolved to resist him steadfast in the faith. Accordingly, though I was exceedingly sick in reading the prayers, and almost unable to speak when I entered the pulpit, yet God gave me courage to begin, and before I had done, I waxed warm and strong in the Spirit, and offered Jesus Christ freely.[27]

In 1739, in Basingstoke, England, Whitefield preached for an hour in a large room thronged with people, while a mob outside shouted and threw stones at the windows. He recounted, "After this, my spirits revived, my body was strengthened, and God gave me utterance, so that I spoke freely . . . the Word of God."[28] Examples like these serve to demonstrate the energizing effect of the Spirit upon Whitefield's preaching ministry as he faithfully proclaimed the saving message of Christ even amid such adversaries.

DIVINELY COMFORTED

Whitefield was inwardly consoled in the midst of many demanding circumstances in his life and ministry. He was confronted with many difficulties throughout his life and was met by resistance on many sides. Any of these would have been sufficient to have discouraged the strongest of men. Yet, as we read of Whitefield's life, we see a servant of the Lord not deflated by discouragements, nor drowning in despair, but abounding in joy and filled with peace. This must be attributed to the sufficiency of the Holy Spirit within him.

At times, Whitefield felt abandoned by the Lord. It was then that the Lord came in great power to shore up his weakness. Whitefield reflected, "Sometimes I perceive myself deserted for a little while, and much oppressed, especially before preaching, but comfort soon after flows in."[29] The refrain "I was deserted before I went up to the pulpit" was often repeated by Whitefield, but was inevitably followed by "God strengthened me to speak."[30] It was Whitefield's realization of his own weakness that caused him to depend upon God exclusively for His all-sustaining power.

As Whitefield so aptly stated, "I walk continually in the comforts of the Holy Ghost."[31] He received constant encouragement from the Comforter, without whom he could have never continued with calmness of heart in the midst of the many turbulent storms. On one challenging occasion, he remarked, "My soul was full of ineffable comfort and joy in the Holy Ghost."[32] Whitefield found the Holy Spirit to be an endless source of joy in the many disappointments he faced.

In 1738, he boarded the *Mary*, bound from Charleston to England. Except for two or three days, the first month of the passage home was a continuous storm on the open sea. During the first week, Whitefield never undressed, and lay upon the deck, or on a chest every night. On October 3, when they had sailed about 150 miles, they encountered a violent storm, which slit nearly all the ship's sails. The captain's hammock in the great cabin was half-filled with water. Whitefield, in his berth, was drenched. Most of the fresh provisions were washed overboard and the tackling of the ship was seriously injured.[33]

In the midst of such a turbulent storm, Whitefield was kept at peace by the comforting and sustaining presence of the Holy Spirit. He wrote: "I have been but a little sea-sick; and though I have not had my clothes off, and lay upon deck or on a chest every night, yet the goodness of God keeps me healthy and strong, and gives me a feeling possession of His Holy Spirit."[34] It was the Spirit who gave him calm confidence during these most adverse circumstances.

Whitefield understood that the inward ministry of the Spirit, though inexplicable, was nevertheless real. Once when he was depleted, he stated, "Afterwards found my strength renewed, and my soul filled with divine love and joy in the Holy Ghost. Oh what a mystery is the hidden life of a Christian."[35] As he faced these many trials in his life and ministry—the conflict with the Wesleys, the financial burden of the Bethesda Orphanage, the long ocean voyages, the premature death of his newborn son, the loss of his wife, and the growing hecklers in the crowd—this valiant soldier of the cross found supernatural solace in the Lord, mediated by the Holy Spirit. Without this inner joy and peace, the multitudes would have not been attracted to the gospel he held forth.

This testimony of such divine help was his constant

refrain. In his *Journals*, Whitefield bore witness, time and again, that it was the Holy Spirit who was granting supernatural peace and joy to his troubled soul: "We long since knew that the Kingdom of God did not consist in any externals, but in righteousness, and peace, and joy in the Holy Ghost."[36] Again, "Glory be to God that He fills me continually, not only with peace, but also joy in the Holy Ghost."[37] Or, "God fills me with love, peace, and joy in the Holy Ghost. . . . Oh how does the Holy Ghost cause me to joy in God!"[38] Whitefield found the Spirit to be a fountain of inexhaustible grace that washed over his weary heart, comforting, upholding, and sustaining him with each laborious step of his extensive journey.

SUPERNATURALLY EFFECTIVE

Whitefield understood that the effects of his preaching were sovereignly determined by God. His responsibility was to deliver the message and leave the results entirely with God. In the wake of Whitefield's preaching, lives were visibly affected and dramatically altered. These results were clearly the effect of God's hand. Iain Murray observed, "Whitefield's preaching was accompanied by effects similar to those produced by the preaching of the apostolic age."[39] J. C. Ryle remarked, "He was one of the most powerful and effective preachers that ever lived."[40] These men understood this effect was the direct result of God's power in Whitefield's ministry.

From the beginning of his ministry, Whitefield recounted

the evidence of the Holy Spirit upon his preaching. After his first sermon, on June 30, 1736, in Gloucester, he wrote, "I was enabled to speak with some degree of gospel authority. Some few mocked, but most for the present seemed struck; and I have since heard, that a complaint has been made to the bishop, that I drove fifteen mad the first sermon. The worthy prelate, as I am informed, wished that the madness might not be forgotten before next Sunday."[41] Even in his initial sermon, Whitefield recognized the supernatural effect upon his listeners.

Later, in Scotland, Whitefield recounted, "The Holy Spirit seemed to come down like a rushing mighty wind. . . . Every day I hear of some fresh good wrought by the power of God. I scarce know how to leave Scotland."[42] Wherever he went, the effect of the Spirit in his ministry was noticeable in the conviction and conversion of souls.

Untold examples could be offered of these Spirit-generated effects. On July 19, 1740, George Whitefield wrote in his *Journals* concerning the effectiveness of his ministry in Charleston, South Carolina: "Indeed, the Word often came like a hammer and a fire."[43] Whitefield attributed this power in preaching to the Holy Spirit. He realized his sermons contained converting power that must be traced back to God. A. S. Billingsley noted:

When Mr. Whitefield preached in New York with "crying, weeping, and wailing" all over the congregation, a little boy sitting on the pulpit stairs was so deeply affected, "that he could scarce stand." He cried out when one asked him why he cried, he said, "Who can help it? The Word cut me to the heart." When he preached in Baskinridge he says, "I had not discoursed long till in every part of the congregation somebody began to cry out, and almost all were melted to tears."[44]

On another occasion, Billingsley explained, "Whitefield gave a word of exhortation with a most melting effect. One that received Christ cried out, 'He is come! He is come!' and could scarce sustain the discovery that Jesus Christ made to his soul."[45] Yet again, Whitefield recorded:

Others were so earnest for the discovery of the Lord Jesus to their souls, that their eager crying obliged me to stop, and I prayed over them as I saw their agonies and distress increase. At length my own soul was so full, that I retired, and was in a strong agony for some time. I wept under a deep sense of my own vileness, and the sovereignty and greatness of God's everlasting love.[46]

Whitefield knew this operation of the Spirit could not be automatically transferred into print. When asked for a copy of a sermon so it might be published, he said, "I have no objection, if you will print the lightning, thunder and rainbow with it."[47]

With humble recognition, Whitefield saw himself as merely a channel through which the Spirit flowed: "The Holy Ghost so powerfully worked upon my hearers, pricking their hearts, and melting them into such floods of tears, that a spiritual man said, 'he never saw the like before.' God is with me. . . . My understanding is more enlightened, my affections more inflamed, and my heart is full of love towards God and man."[48] This is the only explanation that can rightly interpret Whitefield's preaching—it was by the Spirit's operation in his own life and upon his listeners, producing extraordinary effects.

■ ■ ■

The same Spirit who indwelled Whitefield has taken up His royal residence within the heart of every believer in Christ. The same Spirit who called Whitefield from obscurity to worldwide influence has placed the same call upon every Christian's heart to bear gospel witness. The same Spirit who empowered Whitefield in his numerous endeavors will propel every follower of Christ to service in His name. The same Spirit who energized Whitefield will give divine energy and supernatural power today to accomplish all He wills.

It is this influence of the Holy Spirit seen in Whitefield's preaching that so desperately needs to be recovered again. Concerning such Spirit-emboldened preaching, Robert Philip wrote:

It is high time that the church of Christ should consider, not only the duty of depending on the Spirit, but also the import and the importance of the "demonstration of the Spirit," in preaching. That is more than the demonstration of orthodoxy. It is more than the demonstration of either sound scholarship or hard study. It is even more than the demonstration of mere sincerity and fidelity. Sincerity may be cold, and fidelity harsh.[49]

A dead orthodoxy will never impart life in gospel ministry. To the contrary, the power of the Holy Spirit is essential in gospel preaching to inject life to human souls. Whitefield was certainly endued with such divine power in his evangelistic preaching. This heaven-sent power must be recovered in pulpits today. May the sovereign Head of the church, who possesses all authority in heaven and earth, give to His church such Spirit-endowed messengers.

We Want Again Whitefields!

Have we read or heard of any person who called so many thousands, so many myriads of sinners to repentance? Above all, have we read or heard of anyone who has been God's blessed instrument to bring so many sinners from darkness to light and from the power of Satan unto God as Whitefield?[1]

—JOHN WESLEY

It is virtually impossible to read the life and ministry of George Whitefield without being impressed with his evangelistic zeal. Here is a man who gave himself entirely to the most noble calling of all—preaching for the souls of men. Without gimmicks and props, without smoke and mirrors, here is a humble messenger, armed only with the gospel, emboldened by the Spirit, seeking to revive the church and win the lost to Christ. Here is a soul on fire and a life zealous to preach the glorious gospel.

129

Whitefield never lost sight of the fact that he was a lowly sinner saved by the matchless grace of his Redeemer. He never promoted himself, but desired simply that Christ be glorified through his many labors. He allowed no Christian institution or religious movement to be named after him. He was a model of self-effacing humility, even amid his painful controversies. He never championed his own cause, nor sought the spotlight. Instead, Whitefield only sought the honor of God in the salvation of lost souls.

What do we learn most from the life of George Whitefield? Among his many qualities worth emulating, we see the primacy of the gospel in his preaching. He lived to proclaim the saving message of Jesus Christ. In this present day when many in ministry are striving to be many things—CEOs, marketers, strategists, communicators, actors, dramatists, organizers, promoters, and the like—what a challenge it is to be brought face-to-face with one like Whitefield.

This is what must be recovered in this present day. Charles Spurgeon prophetically described the great need of the hour:

We want again Luthers, Calvins, Bunyans, Whitefields, men fit to mark eras, whose names breathe terror in our foemen's ears. We have dire need of such. Whence will they come to us? They are the gifts of Jesus Christ to the church, and will come in due time. He has power to give us back again a golden age of preachers, and when the good old truth is once more preached by men whose lips are touched as with a live coal from off the altar, this shall be the instrument in the hand of the Spirit for bringing about a great and thorough revival of religion in the land. [2]

With unwavering conviction, Spurgeon concluded:

I do not look for any other means of converting men beyond the simple preaching of the gospel and the opening of men's ears to hear it. The moment the church of God shall despise the pulpit, God will despise her. It has been through the ministry that the Lord has always been pleased to review and bless His churches.[3]

The enduring example of this "Grand Itinerant" sets before us what should be in every preacher's soul. In his magisterial work on George Whitefield, Arnold Dallimore longed for what is surely in our hearts:

This book is written in the desire—perhaps in a measure of inner certainty—that we shall see the great Head of the Church once more bring into being His special instruments of revival, that He will again raise up unto Himself certain young men whom He may use in this glorious employ. And what manner of men will they be? Men mighty in the Scriptures, their lives dominated by a sense of the greatness, the majesty and holiness of God, and their minds and hearts aglow with the great truths of the doctrines of grace. They will be men who have learned what it is to die to self, to human aims and personal ambitions; men who are willing to be "fools for Christ's sake," who will bear reproach and falsehood, who will labour and suffer, and whose supreme desire will be, not to gain earth's accolades, but to win the Master's approbation when they appear before His awesome judgment seat. They will be men who will preach with broken hearts and tear-filled eyes, and upon whose ministries God will grant an extraordinary effusion of the Holy Spirit. . . . Indeed this book goes forth with the earnest prayer that, amidst the rampant iniquity and glaring apostasy of the twentieth century God will use it toward the raising up of such men and toward the granting of a mighty revival such as was witnessed two hundred years ago.[4]

May the Lord raise up a new generation of zealous evangelists who will never lose sight of the need to preach the gospel with urgency and passion. Now more than ever, we must have men dominated by the glory of God who will expound the Scripture, proclaim the doctrines of grace, and call men and women to follow Christ by faith. May the Lord grant to preachers and Christians alike the mind, heart, and passion of George Whitefield—a mind for the truth, a heart for the world, and a passion for the glory of God.

Truly, we want again Whitefields!

NOTES

Preface: Lightning from a Cloudless Sky

1. Iain H. Murray, *Heroes* (Edinburgh: Banner of Truth, 2009), 53.
2. Martyn Lloyd-Jones, *The Puritans: Their Origins and Successors* (Edinburgh: Banner of Truth, 1996), 107.
3. Murray, *Heroes*, 49.

Chapter One: A Force for the Gospel

1. *C. H. Spurgeon Autobiography, Vol. 2* (London: Passmore and Alabaster, 1898), 66.
2. Whitefield, Letter 110, *The Works of the Reverend George Whitefield, Vol. I* (London: Edward and Charles Dilly, 1771), 105.
3. W. Cooper, "Mr. Cooper's Preface to the Reader," *The Works of Jonathan Edwards, Vol. 2*, revised and corrected by Edward Hickman (1834, repr.; Edinburgh: Banner of Truth, 1979), 258.
4. John Newton, quoted by J. B. Wakeley, *Anecdotes of the Rev. George Whitefield* (1879, repr.; Weston Rhyn, England: Quinta, 2003), 20.
5. Augustus Toplady, "A Concise Character of the Late Rev. Mr. Whitefield," in *The Works of Augustus Toplady, B.A.* (London: J. Chidley, 1837), 494.
6. J. C. Ryle, *The Christian Leaders of the Last Century* (1868, repr.; Moscow, Ida.: Charles Nolan, 2002), 44.
7. *C. H. Spurgeon's Autobiography, Vol. II* (1898, repr.; Pasadena, Tex.: Pilgrim, 1992), 66.
8. Ian R. K. Paisley, "George Whitefield—Or From Pub to Pulpit: A Sermon Preached on the 250th Anniversary of Whitefield's Birth" (Belfast: Puritan, 1964), 1.
9. Martyn Lloyd-Jones, *The Puritans: Their Origins and Successors* (Edinburgh: Banner of Truth, 1996), 104, 111.
10. Paisley, "George Whitefield," 1.
11. Edwin Charles Dargan, *A History of Preaching, Volume II* (Grand Rapids, Mich.: Baker, 1974), 307.
12. Michael A. G. Haykin, *The Revived Puritan* (Dundas, Ontario: Joshua, 2000), 33. [Harry S. Stout, "Heavenly Comet," *Christian History*, 38 (1993), 13.]
13. Lloyd-Jones, *Puritans*, 105.
14. Lloyd-Jones, *Puritans*, 106.
15. Arnold A. Dallimore, *George Whitefield: God's Anointed Servant in the Great Revival of the Eighteenth Century* (Wheaton, Ill.: Crossway, 1990), 17.

16. Ibid., 17.

17. *George Whitefield's Journals* (1738–1741, repr.; Edinburgh: Banner of Truth, 1998), 58.

18. *George Whitefield's Letters* (1771, repr.; Edinburgh: Banner of Truth, 1976), 16.

19. *Whitefield's Journals*, 80.

20. *Whitefield's Journals*, 89, 83.

21. George Whitefield as quoted by Robert Philip, *The Life and Times of George White-field* (1837, repr.; Edinburgh: Banner of Truth, 2007), 103–104.

22. *Whitefield's Journals*, 260–277.

23. *Whitefield's Journals*, 277.

24. Whitefield, Letter 300, in *The Works of the Reverend George Whitefield, Vol. I* (London: Edward and Charles Dilly, 1771), 277.

25. Whitefield, Letter 1414, in *The Works of the Reverend George Whitefield, Vol. III* (London: Edward and Charles Dilly, 1771), 387.

26. *Whitefield's Journals*, 227.

27. Whitefield, Letter 1004 (cf. Letter 1389, 372), in *Works, Vol. III*, 42.

28. Arnold Dallimore, *George Whitefield: The Life and Times of the Great Evangelist of the 18th Century Revival, Vol. 1* (1970, repr.; Edinburgh: Banner of Truth, 1995), 268.

29. Haykin, *The Revived Puritan*, 33–34. [*The Journal of the Rev. John Wesley, A.M.,* ed. Nehemiah Curnock (1911 ed.; repr. London: Epworth, 1960), II, 256–257, n.1.]

30. Andrew A. Bonar, *Memoir and Remains of Robert Murray M'Cheyne* (1844, repr.; Edinburgh: Banner of Truth, 2009), 146.

31. Lloyd-Jones, *Puritans*, 110.

32. J. I. Packer, "The Spirit with the Word: The Reformational Revivalism of George Whitefield," in *The Bible, the Reformation and the Church: Essays in Honor of James Atkinson*, ed. W. P. Stephens (Sheffield, England: Sheffield Academic, 1995), 167.

33. *Benjamin Franklin's Autobiography and Selected Writings,* ed. Dixon Wecter and Larzer Ziff (New York: Holt, Rinehart and Winston, 1967), 110.

34. Walter Isaacson, *Benjamin Franklin: An American Life* (New York: Simon and Schuster, 2003), 111.

35. Amos Stevens Billingsley, *The Life of the Great Preacher, Reverend George Whitefield: Prince of Pulpit Orators and Specimens of His Sermons* (1878, repr., Charleston, S.C.: Nabu, 2010), 180.

36. *Whitefield's Journals,* 477.

37. Jonathan Edwards, as quoted in *The Cambridge Companion to Jonathan Edwards*, ed. Stephen J. Stein (New York: Cambridge, 2007), 137.

38. Perry Miller, *Jonathan Edwards* (New York: William Sloan Associates, 1949), 134.

39. Billingsley, *The Life of the Great Preacher*, 187.

40. Wakeley, *Anecdotes*, 61.

41. Whitefield, Letter 1170, in *Works, Vol. III*, 208.

42. Dallimore, *George Whitefield: God's Anointed Servant*, 196.

43. Mr. M'Cullock, quoted by Robert Philip, *The Life and Times*, 376.

44. Whitefield, Letter 547, in *Works, Vol. II*, 52.

45. Whitefield, Letter 784, in *Works, Vol. II*, 289.

46. *The Journal of John Wesley* (Chicago: Moody, 1974), 284.

47. John Gillies, *Memoirs of George Whitefield* (New Haven, Conn.: Whitmore and Buckingham and H. Mansfield: 1834), 216.

48. Sir Marcus Loane, *Oxford and the Evangelical Succession* (Ross-shire, Scotland: Christian Focus, 2007), 55.

49. John Wesley, *Sermons on Several Occasions, Volume 1* (London: Printed for Thomas Tegg, 73, Cheapside, 1829), 596.

50. J. C. Ryle, "George Whitefield and His Ministry," in *Select Sermons of George Whitefield*, ed. J. C. Ryle (1958, repr.; Edinburgh: Banner of Truth, 1997), 32.

Chapter Two: A Life of Singular Devotion

1. Lloyd-Jones, *Puritans,* 104–105.

2. J. C. Ryle, *Select Sermons of George Whitefield* (1958, repr.; Edinburgh: Banner of Truth, 1997), 41.

3. Packer, "The Spirit with the Word," 173.

4. Mark A. Noll, "Pietism," in *Evangelical Dictionary of Theology* (Grand Rapids, Mich.: Baker, 1999), 855–856.

5. *Whitefield's Letters,* 33.

6. E. A. Johnston, *George Whitefield: A Definitive Biography, Vol. 1* (Stoke-on-Trent, England: Tentmaker, 2008), 498.

7. Lloyd-Jones, *Puritans*, 118–119.

8. *Whitefield's Journals,* 48.

9. Dallimore, *George Whitefield: The Life and Times, Vol. 1*, 22.

10. *Whitefield's Journals*, 60.

11. Ibid., 48.

12. Ibid.

13. Dallimore, *George Whitefield: The Life and Times, Vol. 1*, 22.

14. *Whitefield's Journals*, 60.

15. Whitefield, Sermon 2, in *The Works of the Reverend George Whitefield, Vol. V* (London: Edward and Charles Dilly, 1772), 27.

16. Haykin, *The Revived Puritan*, 105.

17. Whitefield, Letter 381, in *Works, Vol. I,* 28.

18. Philip, *The Life and Times,* 565.

19. *Whitefield's Journals*, 83–84.

20. Ibid., 61.

21. Dallimore, *George Whitefield: The Life and Times, Vol. 1*, 80. Law's rules are a set of

guidelines for holy living formulated by the English minister and teacher William Law and published in 1729.

22. Whitefield, Sermon 2, in *Works, Vol. V*, 28.

23. *Whitefield's Journals*, 91.

24. Ibid.

25. Whitefield, Letter 35, in *Works, Vol. I*, 38.

26. Whitefield, Sermon 2, in *Works, Vol. V*, 28.

27. Lloyd-Jones, *Puritans,* 127.

28. Whitefield, Sermon 31, in *Works, Vol. V*, 457.

29. Stephen Mansfield, *Forgotten Founding Father: The Heroic Legacy of George White-field* (Nashville: Cumberland House, 2001), 214, 216.

30. *Sermons of George Whitefield* (Peabody, Mass.: Hendrickson, 2009), 199–200.

31. Ibid., 199–200.

32. *Whitefield's Journals*, 347–348.

33. Whitefield, Letter 262, in *Works, Vol. I*, 245.

34. Whitefield, Letter 120, in *Works, Vol. I*, 115.

35. Lloyd-Jones, *Puritans*, 106.

36. Ryle, *Select Sermons*, 5–6.

37. Whitefield, Letter 267, in *Works, Vol. I*, 250.

38. Whitefield, Letter 271, in *Works, Vol. I*, 255.

39. Gillies, *Memoirs* (Whitmore), 216–219.

40. Whitefield, Letter 991, in *Works, Vol. III*, 29.

41. Arnold Dallimore, *George Whitefield: The Life and Times of the Great Evangelist of the 18th Century Revival, Vol. 2* (Edinburgh: Banner of Truth, 1995), 258.

42. Ryle, *Select Sermons*, 39.

43. Whitefield, Letter 1102, in *Works, Vol. III*, 144.

44. Haykin, *The Revived Puritan*, 103.

45. Whitefield, Letter 298, in *Works, Vol. I*, 275.

46. *Whitefield's Journals*, 462.

47. Whitefield, Letter 640, in *The Works of the Reverend George Whitefield, Vol. II* (London: Edward and Charles Dilly, 1771), 144.

48. Whitefield, Letter 68, in *Works, Vol. I*, 66.

49. Whitefield, Letter 52, in *Works, Vol. I*, 55.

50. Whitefield, Letter 66, in *Works, Vol. I*, 64.

51. *Whitefield's Journals*, 17.

52. Lee Gatiss, introduction to *The Sermons of George Whitefield, Part 1*, edited and with an introduction by Lee Gatiss (Wheaton, Ill.: Crossway, 2012), 29.

53. Whitefield, Letter 29, in *Works, Vol. I*, 33.

54. Ryle, *Select Sermons*, 5.

55. Whitefield, Letter 1017, in *Works, Vol. III*, 56.

56. Whitefield, Sermon 32, in *The Works of the Reverend George Whitefield, Vol. VI* (London: Edward and Charles Dilly, 1771), 6–7.

57. Ibid., 7.

58. *Whitefield's Journals*, 61.

59. Ibid.

Chapter Three: A Theology of Sovereign Grace

1. Dallimore, *George Whitefield: The Life and Times, Vol. 1*, 409.

2. Packer, "The Spirit with the Word: The Reformational Revivalism of George Whitefield," 173.

3. Gatiss, introduction to *Sermons of George Whitefield, Part 1*, 32.

4. Mark A. Noll, *Biographical Entries from Evangelical Dictionary of Theology, Vol. 1* (Grand Rapids, Mich.: Baker, 1997, 1984), 1273.

5. Whitefield, Letter 458, in *Works, Vol. I*, 442.

6. Ibid., 205.

7. Johnston, *George Whitefield: A Definitive Biography, Vol. I*, 498.

8. Ibid.

9. Whitefield, Letter 92, in *Works, Vol. I*, 88.

10. Whitefield in Gillies, *Memoirs of Rev. George Whitefield* (Middletown, Conn.: Hunt and Noyes, 1839), 95.

11. Packer, "The Spirit with the Word," 180.

12. *The Works of the Reverend George Whitefield, Vol. IV* (London: Edward and Charles Dilly, 1772), 247.

13. R. Elliot, "A Summary of Gospel Doctrine Taught by Mr. Whitefield," in *Select Sermons of George Whitefield* (1958, repr.; Edinburgh: The Banner of Truth Trust, 1997), 52–53.

14. Whitefield in Gillies, *Memoirs* (Hunt and Noyes), 247.

15. *Sermons of George Whitefield*, 235.

16. Ibid., 234.

17. Johnston, *George Whitefield: A Definitive Biography, Vol. I*, 503.

18. *Sermons of George Whitefield*, 235.

19. Ibid.

20. Ibid.

21. Ibid., 72.

22. Ibid., 235.

23. Ibid., 72–73.

24. Haykin, *The Revived Puritan*, 45. [Tyerman, Life, II, 242.]

25. *Sermons of George Whitefield*, 234.

26. Elliot, *Select Sermons*, 57.

27. Whitefield in Gillies, *Memoirs* (Hunt and Noyes), 366.

28. Whitefield, Sermon 44: "Christ the Believer's Wisdom, Righteousness, Sanctification, and Redemption," in *Works, Vol. VI*, 188–189.

29. Whitefield in Gillies, *Memoirs* (Hunt and Noyes), 599.

30. Ibid., 366.

31. Whitefield, Sermon 44: "Christ the Believer's Wisdom, Righteousness, Sanctification, and Redemption," in *Works, Vol. VI*, 188–189.

32. Elliot, *Select Sermons*, 69.

33. Whitefield in Gillies, *Memoirs* (Hunt and Noyes), 629–630.

34. Gatiss, introduction to *The Sermons of George Whitefield, Part 1*, 33.

35. Whitefield in Gillies, *Memoirs* (Hunt and Noyes), 641.

36. Whitefield, Sermon 38, in *Works, Vol. VI*, 92.

37. Whitefield, "The Farewell Sermon," in *Select Sermons of George Whitefield* (1958, repr.; Edinburgh: Banner of Truth, 1997), 190.

38. *Select Sermons of George Whitefield,* 62.

39. Gatiss, introduction to *The Sermons of George Whitefield, Part 1*, 33.

40. Whitefield, Sermon 61: "The Good Shepherd," in *The Sermons of George Whitefield, Part 2*, edited and with an introduction by Lee Gatiss (Stoke-on-Trent, England: Tentmaker, 2010), 455.

41. Whitefield, Sermon 35, in *Works, Vol. VI* , 62.

42. Whitefield, "On Regeneration," in *Sermons of George Whitefield, Part 2*, 276.

43. Elliot, *Select Sermons*, 54.

44. Ibid.

45. Whitefield, Sermon 35, in *Works, Vol. V,* 61.

46. Whitefield, Sermon 35, in *Works, Vol. VI* , 61.

47. Whitefield, Sermon 39, in *Works, Vol. VI*, 123–124.

48. Elliot, *Select Sermons*, 56.

49. *Sermons of George Whitefield,* 333.

50. Ibid., 334.

51. *Whitefield's Journals*, 581.

52. *Sermons of George Whitefield,* 334.

53. Ibid.

54. Whitefield, as quoted in Haykin, *The Revived Puritan*, 107.

55. *Whitefield's Journals*, 578.

56. Stephen Mansfield, *Forgotten Founding Father: The Heroic Legacy of George Whitefield* (Nashville: Highland, 2001), 156.

57. Ibid., 261.

58. Ibid.

59. George Whitefield, as quoted by Dallimore, *George Whitefield: God's Anointed Servant*, 69–70.

Chapter Four: A Gospel without Compromise

1. John Newton, as quoted by J. R. Andrews, *George Whitefield: A Light Rising in Obscurity* (London: Morgan & Chase, 1864), 389.
2. Lloyd-Jones, *Puritans,* 120.
3. *Sermons of George Whitefield* (Peabody, Mass.: Hendrickson, 2009), 284.
4. Whitefield, Sermon 35, in *The Works of the Reverend George Whitefield, Vol. VI* (London: Edward and Charles Dilly, 1772), 60–61.
5. *Sermons of George Whitefield*, 222.
6. Whitefield, Sermon 44, in *Works, Vol. VI*, 200.
7. *Sermons on Important Subjects by the Rev. George Whitefield* (London: B. Fisher, 1841), 57.
8. Whitefield, Sermon 35, in *Works, Vol. VI*, 62.
9. *Sermons of George Whitefield*, 110.
10. Whitefield, Sermon 35, in *Works, Vol. VI*, 60.
11. *George Whitefield's Journals* (1738–1741, repr.; Edinburgh: Banner of Truth, 1998), 495.
12. Joseph Belcher, *George Whitefield: A Biography with Special Reference to His Labors in America* (New York: American Tract Society, 1857), 514.
13. Lloyd-Jones, *Puritans*, 120.
14. As quoted in Sinclair B. Ferguson, *In Christ Alone: Living the Gospel Centered Life* (Orlando, Fla.: Reformation Trust, 2007), 127.
15. Arnold A. Dallimore, *George Whitefield: The Life and Times of the Great Evangelist of the 18th Century Revival, Vol. 1* (Edinburgh: Banner of Truth, 1970), 127–128.
16. Dallimore, *Whitefield: Life and Times, Vol. 1*, 345. Dallimore also notes that through his interaction with Archbishop Tillotson (see below), Whitefield "focused the attention of thousands on the great central truth of the revival: the necessity of the new birth" (p. 483).
17. Dallimore, *Whitefield: Life and Times, Vol. 1*, 124.
18. Ibid., 345.
19. George Whitefield, Samuel Drew and Joseph Smith, "Sermons on Important Subjects," in *Commendations by Notable Preachers, the Works of George Whitefield* (Weston Rhyn, England: Quinta [First published 1825] 2000), 31.
20. Harry S. Stout, "Whitefield in Three Countries," in *Evangelicalism: Comparative Studies of Popular Protestantism in North America, The British Isles, and Beyond, 1700–1900,* ed. Mark A. Noll, David Bebbington, and George A. Rawlyk (New York: Oxford University Press, 1994), 58–59. "His product—the New Birth—he would market . . . in the public square . . ."
21. Whitefield, Sermon 49, in *Works, Vol. VI*, 257.
22. Billingsley, *The Life of the Great Preacher*, 136.
23. Whitefield, Sermon 49, in *Works, Vol. VI*, 259.
24. Whitefield, Sermon 41, in *Works, Vol. VI*, 149.

25. Ibid.

26. George Whitefield, as quoted by Sir Marcus Loane, *Oxford and the Evangelical Succession* (London: Butterworth, 1950), 41.

27. Lloyd-Jones, *Puritans*, 125.

28. Ibid., 126.

29. Lee Gatiss, introduction to *The Sermons of George Whitefield, Vol. 1*, edited and with an introduction by Lee Gatiss (Wheaton, Ill.: Crossway, 2012), 22.

30. Whitefield, Sermon 32, in *Works, Vol. VI*, 18. Emphasis added.

31. Whitefield, Sermon 51, in *Works, Vol. VI*, 298. Emphasis added.

32. *Sermons of George Whitefield*, 159. Emphasis added.

33. Whitefield, Sermon 36, in *Works, Vol. VI*, 78.

34. Whitefield, Sermon 22, in *The Works of the Reverend George Whitefield, Vol. V* (London: Edward and Charles Dilly, 1772), 325–326.

35. Whitefield, Sermon 35, in *Works, Vol. VI*, 60. Emphasis added.

36. Whitefield, Sermon 36, in *Works, Vol. VI*, 77–78.

37. J. I. Packer, "The Spirit with the Word: The Reformational Revivalism of George Whitefield," in *The Bible, the Reformation and the Church,* ed. W. P. Stephens (Sheffield, England: Sheffield Academic, 1995), 186.

38. *Sermons of George Whitefield*, 228.

39. Whitefield, Sermon 29, in *Works, Vol. V*, 428.

40. Whitefield, Sermon 28, in *Works, Vol. V*, 426.

41. *Sermons of George Whitefield*, 154.

42. Billingsley, *The Life of the Great Preacher*, 149.

43. Ibid., 149.

44. Arnold Dallimore, *George Whitefield: The Life and Times of the Great Evangelist of the 18th Century Revival, Vol. 2* (Edinburgh: Banner of Truth, 1995), 122.

45. Arnold Dallimore, "George Whitefield," in *New Dictionary of Theology*, eds. Sinclair Ferguson and David Wright (Downers Grove, Ill.: InterVarsity Press, 1988), 721.

Chapter Five: A Passion That Consumed

1. Ryle, "George Whitefield and His Ministry," in *Select Sermons,* 21.

2. Dallimore, *George Whitefield: The Life and Times*, 541.

3. Nathan Cole, as quoted by Iain H. Murray, *Jonathan Edwards: A New Biography* (Edinburgh: Banner of Truth, 1987), 214.

4. Ibid.

5. Nathan Cole, *Spiritual Travels,* as quoted in *Whitefield's Journals*, 562.

6. Ryle, "George Whitefield and His Ministry," in *Select Sermons*, 36.

7. Whitefield, "Neglect of Christ," in Gillies, *Memoirs* (Whitmore), 590.

8. Edward S. Ninde, *George Whitefield: Prophet-Preacher* (New York: Abingdon, 1924), 176–177.

NOTES

9. R. Kent Hughes, *Romans: Righteousness from Heaven* (Wheaton, Ill.: Crossway, 1991), xii.

10. Gillies, *Memoirs* (Whitmore), 273–274.

11. Ryle, "George Whitefield and His Ministry," in *Select Sermons*, 36.

12. Paisley, "George Whitefield," 10–11.

13. Whitefield, Letter 733, in *Works, Vol. II*, 230.

14. Whitefield, Letter 412, in *Works, Vol. I*, 387.

15. Paisley, "George Whitefield," 11.

16. Ibid.

17. Whitefield, Letter 916, in *Works, Vol. II,* 432.

18. Whitefield, Letter 597, in *Works, Vol. II*, 105.

19. John Carrick, *The Imperative of Preaching* (Edinburgh: Banner of Truth, 2002), 43–44.

20. Packer, "The Spirit with the Word," 180.

21. Billingsley, *The Life of the Great Preacher*, iii.

22. Gillies, *Memoirs* (Whitmore), 24.

23. Ibid.

24. Ibid., 262.

25. John Wesley, quoted by Gillies, *Memoirs* (Whitmore), 244.

26. Ibid., 247.

27. Ibid.

28. Lloyd-Jones, *Puritans*, 117.

29. Philip, *The Life and Times*, 557.

30. Whitefield, quoted by Gillies, *Memoirs* (Whitmore), 274.

31. Ibid., 235–236.

32. Ibid.

33. Ibid., 243.

34. Mansfield, *Forgotten Founding Father*, 124–125.

35. Belcher, *George Whitefield*, 514.

36. Ibid., 351.

37. Gillies, *Memoirs* (Whitmore), 24.

38. Loane, *Oxford and the Evangelical Succession* (Christian Focus), 61.

39. Whitefield, Sermon 38, in *Works, Vol. VI*, 101.

40. *Selected Sermons of George Whitefield* (Philadelphia: Union, 1904), 91.

41. Whitefield, Sermon 22, in *Works, Vol. V*, 325–326.

42. Ibid.

43. Whitefield, Sermon 14, in *Works, Vol. V*, 230.

44. Ryle, *Christian Leaders*, 37.

45. Whitefield, Letter 110, in *Works, Vol. I*, 105.

46. Gillies, *Memoirs* (Whitmore), 243.

47. Thomas S. Kidd, *The Great Awakening: The Roots of Evangelical Christianity in Colonial America* (New Haven, Conn.: Yale, 2007), 61.

48. Ibid.

49. Erskine Clarke, *Our Southern Zion: A History of Calvinism in the South Carolina Low Country, 1690–1990* (Tuscaloosa, Ala.: University of Alabama Press, 1996), 77.

50. Ibid.

51. *The Poems of Phillis Wheatley* (Chapel Hill: University of North Carolina Press, 1989), 134.

52. Harry S. Stout, *The Divine Dramatist: George Whitefield and the Rise of Modern Evangelicalism* (Grand Rapids, Mich.: Eerdmans, 1991), 239–240.

53. Ibid.

54. Whitefield, Sermon 27, in *Works, Vol. V*, 416.

Chapter Six: A Mandate from the Lord

1. Lloyd-Jones, *Puritans*, 126–127.

2. Samuel Davies, as quoted by Lloyd-Jones, *Puritans,* 123–124.

3. Paisley, "George Whitefield," 9.

4. Ibid.

5. Lloyd-Jones, *Puritans*, 119.

6. *Sermons of George Whitefield*, 335.

7. Packer, "The Spirit with the Word," 170.

8. Ibid.

9. Whitefield, Letter 588, in *Works, Vol. II*, 96.

10. J. I. Packer, foreword to *George Whitefield: A Definitive Biography, Vol. 1,* by E. A. Johnston, xvii.

11. Wakeley, *Anecdotes*, 28.

12. Ibid., 29.

13. *Whitefield's Journals*, 200–201.

14. *Whitefield's Journals*, 203.

15. Ibid., 203.

16. Dallimore, *George Whitefield: The Life and Times,* 117.

17. *Whitefield's Journals*, 429.

18. Lloyd-Jones, *Puritans*, 126.

19. Ibid., 126–127.

20. Whitefield, Letter 250, in *Works, Vol. I*, 237.

21. Whitefield, Letter 272, in *Works, Vol. I*, 257.

22. Whitefield, Letter 300, in *Works, Vol. I*, 276.

23. Whitefield, Letter 396, in *Works, Vol. I*, 368.

24. Billingsley, *The Life of the Great Preacher*, 185.

25. Whitefield, Letter 312, in *Works, Vol. I*, 388.

26. Whitefield, Letter 544, in *Works, Vol. II*, 47.

27. *Whitefield's Journals*, 206.

28. Ibid., 211.

29. Ibid., 195.

30. Ibid., 462.

31. Philip, *The Life and Times,* 248.

32. *Whitefield's Journals*, 210.

33. Ibid., 167–180.

34. Ibid., 166.

35. Ibid., 251.

36. Ibid., 256.

37. Ibid., 195.

38. Ibid., 201.

39. Murray, *Heroes*, 52.

40. J. C. Ryle, *A Sketch of the Life and Labors of George Whitefield* (New York: Anson D. F. Randolph, 1854), 4.

41. Whitefield, Letter 16, in *Works, Vol. I*, 19.

42. Whitefield, Letter 369, in *Works, Vol. I*, 337.

43. *Whitefield's Journals*, 444.

44. Amos Stevens Billingsley, *The Life of the Great Preacher Reverend George Whitefield* (Philadelphia: P. W. Ziegler, 1878), 183.

45. Ibid.

46. Ibid., 184.

47. Lloyd-Jones, *Puritans*, 122.

48. *Whitefield's Journals*, 197.

49. Philip, *The Life and Times*, 212.

Conclusion: We Want Again Whitefields!

1. *The Works of the Reverend John Wesley, A.M. Vol. 1* (New York: Emory and Waugh, 1831), 477.

2. *C. H. Spurgeon Autobiography, Vol. 1: The Early Years, 1834–1859*, compiled by Susannah Spurgeon and Joseph Harrald (Carlisle, Pa.: Banner of Truth, 1897–1900, 1962), v.

3. Ibid.

4. Dallimore, *George Whitefield: The Life and Times, Vol. 1*, 16.

BIBLIOGRAPHY

Andrews, J. R. *George Whitefield: A Light Rising in Obscurity.* London: Morgan & Chase, 1864.

Belcher, Joseph. *George Whitefield: A Biography with Special Reference to His Labors in America.* New York: American Tract Society, 1857.

Billingsley, Amos Stevens. *The Life of the Great Preacher Reverend George Whitefield.* Philadelphia: P. W. Ziegler, 1878.

———. *The Life of the Great Preacher, Reverend George Whitefield: Prince of Pulpit Orators and Specimens of His Sermons.* 1878. Reprint, Charleston, S.C.: Nabu, 2010.

Bonar, Andrew A. *Memoir and Remains of Robert Murray M'Cheyne.* 1844. Reprint, Edinburgh: Banner of Truth, 2009.

Carrick, John. *The Imperative of Preaching.* Edinburgh: Banner of Truth, 2002.

Clarke, Erskine. *Our Southern Zion: A History of Calvinism in the South Carolina Low Country, 1690–1990.* Tuscaloosa: University of Alabama Press, 1996.

Cooper, W. "Mr. Cooper's Preface to the Reader," in *The Works of Jonathan Edwards, Vol. 2,* revised and corrected by Edward Hickman. 1834. Reprint, Edinburgh: Banner of Truth, 1979.

Dallimore, Arnold. *George Whitefield: God's Anointed Servant in the Great Revival of the Eighteenth Century.* Wheaton, Ill.: Crossway, 1990.

———. "George Whitefield." In *New Dictionary of Theology*, eds. Sinclair Ferguson and David Wright. Downers Grove, Ill.: InterVarsity Press, 1988.

———. *George Whitefield: The Life and Times of the Great Evangelist of the 18th Century Revival, Vol. 1.* 1970. Reprint, Edinburgh: Banner of Truth, 1995.

———. *George Whitefield: The Life and Times of the Great Evangelist of the 18th Century Revival, Vol. 2.* Edinburgh: Banner of Truth, 1995.

Dargan, Edwin Charles. *A History of Preaching, Volume II*. Grand Rapids, Mich.: Baker, 1974.

Elliot, R. *Select Sermons of George Whitefield*. 1958. Reprint, Edinburgh: The Banner of Truth Trust, 1997.

Ferguson, Sinclair B. *In Christ Alone: Living the Gospel Centered Life*. Orlando, Fla.: Reformation Trust, 2007.

Franklin, Benjamin. *Benjamin Franklin's Autobiography and Selected Writings*. Edited by Dixon Wecter and Larzer Ziff. New York: Holt, Rinehart and Winston, 1967.

Gatiss, Lee. Introduction to *The Sermons of George Whitefield, Part 1*, edited and with an introduction by Lee Gatiss. Wheaton, Ill.: Crossway, 2012.

Gillies, John. *Memoirs of Rev. George Whitefield*. Middletown, Conn.: Hunt and Noyes, 1839.

———. *Memoirs of Rev. George Whitefield*. New Haven, Conn.: Whitmore and Buckingham and H. Mansfield: 1834.

Haykin, Michael A. G. *The Revived Puritan*. Dundas, Ontario: Joshua, 2000. [Harry S. Stout. "Heavenly Comet." Christian History, 38 (1993).]

Hughes, R. Kent. *Romans: Righteousness from Heaven*. Wheaton, Ill.: Crossway, 1991.

Johnston, E. A. *George Whitefield: A Definitive Biography, Vol. 1*. Stoke-on-Trent, England: Tentmaker, 2008.

Isaacson, Walter. *Benjamin Franklin: An American Life*. New York: Simon and Schuster, 2003.

Kidd, Thomas S. *The Great Awakening: The Roots of Evangelical Christianity in Colonial America*. New Haven, Conn.: Yale, 2007.

Loane, Sir Marcus. *Oxford and the Evangelical Succession*. London: Butterworth, 1950.

———. *Oxford and the Evangelical Succession*. Ross-shire, Scotland: Christian Focus, 2007.

Lloyd-Jones, Martyn. *The Puritans: Their Origins and Successors*. Edinburgh: Banner of Truth, 1996.

Mansfield, Stephen. *Forgotten Founding Father: The Heroic Legacy of George Whitefield.* Nashville: Cumberland House, 2001.

Miller, Perry. *Jonathan Edwards.* New York: William Sloan Associates, 1949.

Murray, Iain H. *Heroes.* Edinburgh: Banner of Truth, 2009.

———. *Jonathan Edwards: A New Biography.* Edinburgh: Banner of Truth, 1987.

Ninde, Edward S. *George Whitefield: Prophet-Preacher.* New York: Abingdon, 1924.

Noll, Mark A. *Biographical Entries from Evangelical Dictionary of Theology, Vol. 1.* Grand Rapids, Mich.: Baker, 1997, 1984.

———. "Pietism." In *Evangelical Dictionary of Theology* (Grand Rapids, Mich.: Baker, 1999.

Packer, J. I. Foreword to *George Whitefield: A Definitive Biography, Vol. 1,* by E. A. Johnston. Stoke-on-Trent, England: Tentmaker, 2008.

———. "The Spirit with the Word: The Reformational Revivalism of George Whitefield." In *The Bible, the Reformation and the Church: Essays in Honor of James Atkinson*, edited W. P. Stephens. Sheffield, England: Sheffield Academic, 1995.

Paisley, Ian R. K. "George Whitefield—Or From Pub to Pulpit: A Sermon Preached on the 250th Anniversary of Whitefield's Birth." Belfast: Puritan, 1964.

Philip, Robert. *The Life and Times of George Whitefield.* 1837. Reprint, Edinburgh: Banner of Truth, 2007.

Ryle, J. C. *A Sketch of the Life and Labors of George Whitefield.* New York: Anson D. F. Randolph, 1854.

———. "George Whitefield and His Ministry." In *Select Sermons of George Whitefield*, ed. J C. Ryle. 1958. Reprint, Edinburgh: Banner of Truth, 1997.

———. *The Christian Leaders of the Last Century.* 1868. Reprint, Moscow, Ida.: Charles Nolan, 2002.

Spurgeon, Charles H. *C. H. Spurgeon Autobiography, Vol. 1: The Early Years,*

1834–1859, compiled by Susannah Spurgeon and Joseph Harrald. Carlisle, Pa.: Banner of Truth, 1897–1900, 1962.

———. *C. H. Spurgeon Autobiography, Vol. 2*. London: Passmore and Alabaster, 1898.

———. *C. H. Spurgeon's Autobiography, Vol. II*. 1898. Reprint, Pasadena, Tex.: Pilgrim, 1992.

Stein, Stephen J. *The Cambridge Companion to Jonathan Edwards*. New York: Cambridge, 2007.

Stout, Harry S. *The Divine Dramatist: George Whitefield and the Rise of Modern Evangelicalism*. Grand Rapids, Mich.: Eerdmans, 1991.

———. "Whitefield in Three Countries." In *Evangelicalism: Comparative Studies of Popular Protestantism in North America, The British Isles, and Beyond, 1700–1900*. Edited Mark A. Noll, David Bebbington, and George A. Rawlyk. New York: Oxford University Press, 1994.

Toplady, Augustus. "A Concise Character of the Late Rev. Mr. Whitefield," in *The Works of Augustus Toplady, B.A.* London: J. Chidley, 1837.

Wakeley, J. B. *Anecdotes of the Rev. George Whitefield*. 1879. Reprint, Weston Rhyn, England: Quinta, 2003.

Wesley, John. *Sermons on Several Occasions, Volume 1*. London: Printed for Thomas Tegg, 73, Cheapside, 1829.

———. *The Journal of John Wesley*. Chicago: Moody, 1974.

———. *The Works of the Reverend John Wesley, A.M. Vol. 1*. New York: Emory and Waugh, 1831.

Wheatley, Phillis. *The Poems of Phillis Wheatley*. Chapel Hill: University of North Carolina Press, 1989.

Whitefield, George. *George Whitefield's Journals*. 1738–1741. Reprint, Edinburgh: Banner of Truth, 1998.

———. *Selected Sermons of George Whitefield*. Philadelphia: Union, 1904.

———. *Select Sermons of George Whitefield*. 1958. Reprint, Edinburgh: Banner of Truth, 1997.

———. *Sermons of George Whitefield*. Peabody, Mass.: Hendrickson, 2009.

————. *Sermons on Important Subjects by the Rev. George Whitefield.* London: B. Fisher, 1841.

————. *The Sermons of George Whitefield, Part 1.* Edited and with an introduction by Lee Gatiss. Wheaton, Ill.: Crossway, 2012.

————. *The Sermons of George Whitefield, Part 2.* Edited and with an introduction by Lee Gatiss. Stoke-on-Trent, England: Tentmaker, 2010.

————. *The Works of the Reverend George Whitefield, Vol. I.* London: Edward and Charles Dilly, 1771.

————. *The Works of the Reverend George Whitefield, Vol. II.* London: Edward and Charles Dilly, 1771.

————. *The Works of the Reverend George Whitefield, Vol. III.* London: Edward and Charles Dilly, 1771.

————. *The Works of the Reverend George Whitefield, Vol. IV.* London: Edward and Charles Dilly, 1772.

————. *The Works of the Reverend George Whitefield, Vol. V.* London: Edward and Charles Dilly, 1772.

————. *The Works of the Reverend George Whitefield, Vol. VI.* London: Edward and Charles Dilly, 1771.

————. *Whitefield's Letters.* 1771. Reprint, Edinburgh: Banner of Truth, 1976.

Whitefield, George, Samuel Drew, and Joseph Smith, "Sermons on Important Subjects," in *Commendations by Notable Preachers, the Works of George Whitefield.* Weston Rhyn, England: Quinta (First published 1825), 2000.

INDEX

ABOUT THE AUTHOR

D r. Steven J. Lawson is the senior pastor of Christ Fellowship Baptist Church in Mobile, Alabama, having served as a pastor in Arkansas and Alabama for more than thirty years. He is a teaching fellow and board member of Ligonier Ministries, and professor of preaching at The Master's Seminary.

He is a graduate of Texas Tech University (B.B.A.), Dallas Theological Seminary (Th.M.), and Reformed Theological Seminary (D.Min.).

Dr. Lawson is the author of twenty books, his most recent being *In It to Win It: Pursuing Victory in the One Race That Really Counts* and *The Kind of Preaching God Blesses*. His other books include *The Heroic Boldness of Martin Luther*, *Foundations of Grace* and *Pillars of Grace* from the Long Line of Godly Men series; *Famine in the Land: A Passionate Call to Expository Preaching*; *Psalms* volumes 1 and 2 and *Job* in the Holman Old Testament Commentary Series; *Made in Our Image*; and *Absolutely Sure*. His books have been translated into various languages, including Russian, Italian, Portuguese, Spanish, German, Albanian, and Indonesian. He has contributed articles to *Bibliotheca Sacra*, *The Southern Baptist Journal of Theology*, *Faith and Mission*, *Decision* magazine, *Discipleship Journal*, and *Tabletalk*, among other journals and magazines.

Dr. Lawson's pulpit ministry takes him around the world,

including Russia, Ukraine, Wales, England, Germany, Italy, Switzerland, New Zealand, Japan, and to many conferences in the United States, including The Shepherd's Conference and Resolved at Grace Community Church in Sun Valley, California.

He is president of OnePassion Ministries, a ministry designed to bring about biblical reformation in the church today. He serves on the executive board of The Master's Seminary and College, teaches expository preaching at The Master's Seminary in the doctor of ministry program, and hosts The Expositors' Conference at Christ Fellowship Baptist Church. Dr. Lawson has participated in the Distinguished Scholars Lecture Series at The Master's Seminary and serves on the advisory council for Samara Preachers' Institute and Theological Seminary in Samara, Russia.

Dr. Lawson and his wife, Anne, have three sons, Andrew, James, and John, and a daughter, Grace Anne.